From Paris to Alcatraz

From Paris to Alcatraz

The true, untold story of one of the most
notorious con-artists of the twentieth century
– Count Victor Lustig

Betty Jean Lustig and
Nanci Garrett

To order additional copies of this book, contact:
Xlibris Corporation
1-888-795-4274
www.Xlibris.com
Orders@Xlibris.com
99759

Dedication

To Betty Jean, who told me the story but died before she saw it in print.

PROLOGUE

M Y START IN life was as the daughter of a notorious man. He was clever, had a brilliant mind, but used it badly. He was "Count" Victor Lustig.

The Secret Service and the Treasury Department of the United States established one of the greatest man-hunts in their history in search of Victor Lustig. The economy of the United States was threatened because of him. It was not the Secret Service, however, that did the final job. It was an informant, my stepfather, Douglas Conner.

I live with bitter memories. I live trying to recall good ones. I cannot recall not being aware of a life of packing, running, hiding, numerous names and 37 schools; then being dressed in the night to run again. I wasn't ever frightened because I was used to it – from birth.

I had friends stand by when I buried him after he died in prison, but I was truly alone. I had a daughter with me when I buried my mother in a remote area where friends could not be. I had friends stand by, locally and distantly, in their hearts when I buried my husband just a little while ago but what seems to me like years ago.

So, for the enemies of the past and for the friends of the now, I disclose in this book about the life of the man whom I loved every day of my life and who loved me tenderly, the life of my father, Victor Lustig.

– Betty Jean Lustig, 1982

The Road Not Taken

Two roads converged in a yellow wood,
And sorry I could not travel both
And be one traveler, long I stood
And looked down one as far as I could
To where it bent in the undergrowth;

Then took the other, as just as fair,
And having perhaps the better claim,
Because it was grassy and wanted wear;
Thought as for that, the passing there
Had worn them really about the same.

And both that morning equally lay
In leaves no step had trodden black.
Oh! I kept the first for another day;
Yet knowing how way leads to way,
I doubted if I should ever come back.

I shall be telling this with a sign
Somewhere ages and ages hence:
Two roads diverged in a wood, and I –
I took the one less traveled by,
And that has made all the difference.

Robert Frost

INTRODUCTION

"To HELL WITH the government! We're running a race to nowhere and everybody is on the way."

"Who's going to ignite the powder keg? The U.S.A. or the U.S.S.R.?"

The leader of the five men seated around a conference table brought the gavel down forcefully upon the table. The five men came to attention.

"Gentlemen, we are meeting here tonight, not to attack the government of the United States, but to assure its survival, not to abolish government but to improve its performance. Citizens' committee, Citizens for Action, War Resisters, World Federalists, whatever, we are here to act where others are failing."

There was one woman in the group. She sat a little to the right and back of the conference table. No one seemed to know how or why she was there. But the five men, meeting in secret, were not displeased at her presence. It would remove the charge of sexism that would be inevitable when the news of their meeting hit the news media, as they wanted it to do, in time.

"We must abolish the special interest groups that are ruling our country," the gentleman on the right volunteered.

"And the budget that builds arms and starves children," was the comment of the gentleman on the left.

"We need a world order, a system capable of keeping peace and doing away with every possibility of war."

Suggestions continued. One of the men quoted Dwight Eisenhower, "We see as our goal, not a superstate above nations, but a world community, embracing them all, rooted in law and justice and enhancing the potentialities and common purposes of all people."

"We need a world security organization."

"We need to trust one another and quit trying to get ahead."

"We need an antidote to all the hogwash of today's governments."

"We need world order, not just U.S.A."

"We need some means of enforcement, some model the whole world will respect."

"We need to stop the nuclear war hanging over our heads."

"Yes, gentlemen, we need, but how," the Chairman interposed. "How is the question, not need."

"Five men to solve all the problems of the world! Huh!" the dissenter of the group offered.

The lady rose to her feet. "May I speak, gentlemen? May I read to you such a plan as you are suggesting here, a plan to stop war and make peace. It is a peace plan written in 1943." She began reading from a typed draft.

It must be generally conceded that only by the control of the so-called aggressor nations can there be any lasting peace. Experience demonstrates that the total elimination of any nation is, if otherwise desirable, virtually impossible. Then it remains for some plan to be developed whereby aggressive peoples may be effectively prevented from fomenting wars before the initiation of events which make war inevitable.

The following proposal is based upon certain fundamental principles which, notwithstanding their simplicity, are inescapably present in the waging or prevention of all wars.

There is no nation that could wage war without soldiers.
The soldiers are the people.
If left to the people, there would be no wars.

In further consideration of these simple facts, it is the premise of this plan that if put to the vote of the world's population, 98 percent of all people would be against war if they could help it. But under existing conditions, the people have little to say about the actual waging of wars.

It is therefore proposed to place the responsibility squarely on the shoulders of the people – the ones who have to do the actual fighting. The leading nations of the world should sponsor an international law forbidding the individual (on pain of imprisonment) to in any way engage in activities promoting or leading to war. The details of this law should be worked out by experts and could cite specifically such precluded activities as manufacturing implements of war, training for war, et cetera.

The nations should set up an international court to have headquarters in New York, London, Paris, Moscow, and possibly other centers.

The people of all the nations in the world shall be responsible to uphold the peace of the world.

Any person or group of persons who shall conspire against peace of the world shall be punished by the TRIBUNAL OF THE

INTERNATIONAL LAW COURT. Offenses and appropriate punishment would have to be listed after mutual consent.

The organization of this court would require the sponsorship of the three leading nations: Britain, Russia, and the United States and would provide for the ratification of the peoples of all the nations, if they were so disposed. In the event that the people of any nation should approve this law, it would then be compulsory that each nation enforce adherence within its own boundaries. The law must be so constructed that no political group would have the choice of going to war but only the entire people of a nation.

Any war would thus be the responsibility of the people of the world. Certain exceptions could be provided for. International law could forbid agitation of war just as nations now forbid violations of free speech like public teaching of methods of robbing a bank.

In the event that nations might attempt secretly to arm beyond their allocation, any individual might report such infringement secretly by mail to the International Tribunal. Enlisting in any military group, beyond specified bounds, would be a crime, just as desertion is a crime.

The International law as proposed would be quite different from attempts to abrogate war by diplomatic international agreements; the former deals with individuals and the latter with governmental agencies. Under the International Law, any individual participating in war or warlike activities could be held responsible.

There is no individual in the world, except, perhaps, a few fanatics, who would risk the criminal penalties that could be imposed upon him from the outset if he attempted any unspecified military organization. Under this law the individual would be personally responsible and could not hide behind any group and retain his personal immunity.

If it is impossible to pass this International Law, it is impossible to pass laws leading to disarmament or the establishing of any international machinery for abolishing war.

The lady looked up from the paper, "This peace plan, gentlemen, was written by my father, Victor Lustig. I shall go now and let you continue with your meeting."

There was silence at the council table. "It was men and bullets then. It's nations and atoms now."

"Let us adjourn for further consideration at a later date," the chairman said.

"May I ask a question?" a voice from the other end of the table was heard.

"You may."

"Who was Victor Lustig?"

"That's a good question, gentlemen. Who was Victor Lustig? Adjourned."

ONE

W HEN THE STEAMERS began carrying passengers again across the Atlantic after World War I, one passenger who disembarked was a young European traveler in his late 20's, coming to America to look around and perhaps ply a trade that he had intermittently carried on in Europe for several years.

An habitué of Paris and the leading European cities, he was dressed in the latest fashion, with walking stick and Homburg hat, all of which enabled him to invade social circles of a country that was trying to recover from the effects of war. Before the war he had met many rich Americans who fashionably spent their time in European cities, spending money that had finally brought Victor Lustig to the land that produced both friends and money. Many of these Americans became marks for Lustig, but some remained good friends for life.

One of these friends he called Van. Scion of a rich family, he was influential in New York and eastern political circles. Lustig respected him and appreciated his efforts to make him known in the United States. Shortly after his arrival, he had been confined to his hotel room with a severe sinus attack. Van insisted that he go to his country estate to recuperate and had since become his good friend.

Victor Lustig came to America looking around for contacts he could make with rich Americans. He also had rich European friends who were visiting or living in the United States. He visited many cities, meeting people, studying the social world and the underworld, plotting a course that he was not yet sure of himself.

Eventually, he came to Kansas City. The Shannonites and the Pendergast clan were vying for control there. The Kansas City Post was shaking a feeble fist at the powerful Kansas City Star. Victor got himself invited to a party attended by politicians and newspaper men. If he was looking for a mark here, he found an entirely different kind of one. As he entered the party room, his eyes fell upon a magnificent young girl with beautiful red hair and brown eyes that looked directly at him with a milk-white complexion.

Roberta Norét had come to Kansas City from a small Kansas town. After her father's death, she had been taken out of school at the sixth grade and put to work in a laundry by her two maternal half-sisters. A paternal half-sister had rescued her from this child slavery and had taken her to several large cities in her travels and taught her some sophistication. She, however, never returned to school and wore her lack of an education as a cloak of insecurity, despite her beauty and her attempts at sophistication.

She had gone to the party with Lionel Moise, a Kansas City news reporter, but she left that night with Victor Lustig. They eloped to New York and were married there November 3, 1919. As they came to New York, Roberta had said to Victor:

"My dearest friend was killed a year ago tonight by a Brighton train in the Melbone Street tunnel. She was in New York on a vacation. I miss her very much, Vic. Take me to the spot where she was killed."

"Not on our wedding day, indeed," Victor had replied. "That would be too morbid."

"But sometime, Vic, please."

"We'll see," Victor answered uninterested.

The next morning, Lustig's new-made American friend Van called him to his office.

"I think you can help us, Victor."

"Not if it is politics. I'm not interested in politics and, besides, I am preparing to leave for Europe with my bride. We will honeymoon there and she is to meet my father."

Victor made ready to leave. Van was disappointed that he could not secure Vic's help, let alone not even to fully unfold his plan to him.

"You might look into a train accident in a tunnel here that took the life of my wife's friend a year ago. She's very concerned about it," Victor said as he was leaving Van's office.

Van listened with interest. Here was something he wanted to hear.

Al Smith was campaigning for governor of New York. Friday evening, November 1, 1918, he was giving the closing speech of his campaign in Brooklyn. The transit accident which took the life of Roberta's friend happened minutes before his speech. That disaster gave Smith the opening he needed in his close campaign, to prove that his opponent in the election, the incumbent governor, had appointed incompetent people to city jobs and had let politics rule his appointments. He insisted that the accident, which took almost 100 lives and injured many more, was caused by incompetency. The incumbent had allowed old, outmoded, wooden cars to be driven by an inexperienced motorman around a curve at 30 miles an hour, when the speed limit was 6. The Rapid Transit Company made a perfect target for Smith's contention of inefficiency in political appointments.

Mr. Smith was elected governor of New York and his friends were now considering his re-election when Victor and Roberta came to New York to be married. The night before they were to leave on their honeymoon, Van brought three politicians to their hotel room. Discouraged by Victor Lustig's lack of cooperation in his office, he was determined to try again. Here was the situation they laid before 'Count' Victor Lustig. In downstate New York, there was a 'Judge' who wanted Mr. Smith's office. His accusations, begun already against Mr. Smith, were disturbing Mr. Smith's political friends.

"We know that you can secure certain 'papers' in Europe. Help us by doing that now." The 'Judge's' latest scheme was to discredit a Colonel Frederick Stuart Greene, whom Smith had appointed highway commissioner. All along Victor had been listening only half-heartedly to their conversation and schemes. When he heard Frederick Greene's name, he spoke up quickly.

"Repeat that name, please."

It was his friend; he was sure. 'Freddie' was an officer under General Pershing for whom he did invaluable services and who later saved Victor from an arrest.

"Do you know him?" one of the politicians asked.

"I have a slight acquaintance with him," Lustig replied. He wasn't ready to tell his story, but he mentally noted that he would do all he could to clear 'Freddie's' name as the Highway Commissioner of New York.

In his political struggle against Al Smith, the 'Judge' had turned the tables on him. Now it was the 'Judge' accusing him, of incompetent appointments, just as Smith had accused his opponent in the previous campaign. He also turned his ire on Frederick Stuart Greene, Smith's highway commissioner, accusing him of incompetency.

The politicians unfolded their plan. Could Lustig get them some 'papers' in Europe that could be used to discredit the 'Judge'? They knew the 'Judge' was dishonest and they wanted to prove it.

"Now, Governor Smith doesn't know anything about this. He is too honest to take part in any scheming. We don't want anything illegal, just something that will show up the true colors of this 'Judge.'"

Lustig said he would think about it but made no promises. The men had no idea of the complicated scheme 'Count' Victor Lustig would devise and later put before them. He showed the men out the door, eager to return to his bride and plans for the trip.

When the politicians arrived, Roberta had retired to their bedroom to study the many etiquette books she had accumulated since their marriage. Feeling so insecure in this new role as 'Count' Victor Lustig's wife and wanting to make the best wife possible, the little girl from the Kansas country town had bought books on conversations, meals on board ship, fashions, anything that would prepare her to live with this unusual man who was now her husband. She wondered why he married her. He had married her because of her beauty, she decided; he didn't care whether she had brains or not. She never realized the power of her beauty, but he soon found out about the brains behind that beauty.

He knew that after tonight's episode, he would have to educate her or she could ruin him with her ignorance. He would tell her gradually, a bit at a time, the type of life he led. He put his arms around her now, after he had closed the door on the last of the politicians, and held her for quite a while.

"I want you to know, Buckle, (a pet name he had already found for her) that my work is different from any you have known. I'll have to tell you about it each time I take on a new job. So, when we get to Paris, I'll have to be away from you quite a bit because of my work. But you can shop and buy gowns for yourself, for I want my Buckle to look like a queen at all times."

She nodded in her insecurity. She wasn't conscious of her beauty and felt the lack of an education that had been denied her. But she would conquer it. She would become a wife of whom not only Victor could be proud, but his father whom they would see on this trip; the rich merchant of Zurich. She wanted him to be proud of her too, proud that his son had married her. To this end, she read every book she could find about general protocol, table manners, food, wines, ships, and travel. She amazed her husband at the knowledge she had of Zurich and Prague; using maps, city directories, anything to give her information about the habitats of her rich father-in-law.

Despite her cramming for their honeymoon, Roberta still was fearful. She felt that if she did the wrong thing, it would be disastrous for her husband. In her insecurity, she turned to him.

"Vic, I'm so afraid of this trip. Tell me what to do. I haven't traveled as you have and we're going first class. I desperately need your help."

"Don't worry, darling, you will be fine, there will be many other fine ladies on the ship. Just do what they do and you'll be all right."

"Other fine ladies on the ship," he had said. These words put a new fear in her heart. How could 'she' ever compete with 'them' in the eyes of her husband? A wave of jealousy came over her and she threw a dramatic fit.

"If that's the way you are thinking – thinking of all the other fine ladies on the ship; that ends it! I'll throw myself in the ocean and let the fish eat me before I let any other woman take you from me."

He took her in his arms and reassured her that by the time they reached Europe, she would be keeping up with the most experienced travelers, that there was no need to die. It proved true; she did beautifully.

Their honeymoon was all she could have hope for. She had conducted herself perfectly on the ship and now, in Paris, she knew her way around. Victor would drop her off to shop, tell her to take her time and that he would return to pick her up. She never asked where he was going or what he was doing. He would tell her in due time, she thought. Her job now was to become a wife to be proud of, and that way, she thought, was the fashion walk; the exterior Roberta that must be perfect in the eyes of her fastidious husband.

Victor would be gone for a length of time, but she enjoyed spending the money he left her for clothes. Her reading taught her the latest styles and she knew what to buy. However, quite often, most of the money he left with her, she spent on gifts for him.

He would eventually come to pick her up and take her to their hotel rooms where they would spend the evening. He wasn't ready yet to reveal to her the contacts he was making in Paris; ones that he might need to help him if he joined in the crusade to disqualify a 'Judge' and thus exonerate Al Smith and 'Freddie'. The latter was the real reason for his efforts. It would take time but it could be done, he reasoned, as a plan began to unfold in his mind.

Their visit with his father and the introduction of his bride was short, but Roberta was satisfied. He didn't seem as strict as Victor had pictured him. He was exacting, but her job was to come up to these exactions. His patience with her in her inability to speak his language moved her, and in the many times she saw him in later years, she always felt at home with him. "You are a very handsome woman," he told her.

Their visit was cut short. Victor said that they had to go home. It would mean that she wouldn't celebrate her birthday, her first one since their marriage, with Victor's father as they had planned. Roberta was disappointed; she had wanted to celebrate her birthday there and continue it in Paris. She wanted a long celebration with her husband at her side. Instead, they celebrated it in the old Astor Hotel in New York.

Victor still wanted to make it a big celebration, for he sensed her unhappiness about returning so soon from Europe. Van helped by inviting many of his 'theatrical' friends to a party which Victor planned. Roberta had purchased many beautiful gowns in Paris but her favorite for this party was ivory chiffon with a gold lame fitted slip. That was her choice for the night. Many years later, Victor told his daughter that she was a vision of an angel that night. Regretfully, he could never make Roberta realize, completely, how much he loved her; and that what she wore or what she did was not so all-important. Perhaps, if she had realized it, life might have been different for them.

The day after the birthday party, Victor began his planned, slow education of his wife. He explained to her that he would have to work, as all men did, to earn the money that he loved to shower on her. With the ease of a diplomat, he began laying the foundation for the grand announcement: that he was a confidence man and gambled a lot. But he was never dishonest, he would show her. He was just a good gambler. He didn't have to cheat; he was an expert player. She didn't understand and it took another few months to absorb it all. He explained to her, as much as he felt she could accept, about his current business deal now with the New York politicians. He mentioned his friend, 'Freddie', and his desire to exonerate him.

As he walked her back to their living room, he again said that his work was different than any she had known. He had told her that before. What she wanted to know was what, not why.

"All this would not be possible if I did not work. And when I work I must be away from you."

She said she knew that; his work was different, and not all 'legal'.

"My work is not illegal. I simply find people who are doing illegal things already. I merely assist them to further their illegal acts."

According to his reasoning, doing that was not illegal for him. He continued to outline the various means and methods he employed in his work and she, not being quite as ignorant as he had thought, surprised him with what she knew of Kansas City politics.

"Vic, why didn't you tell me on our wedding day that my suit was out of style?"

"I didn't want to hurt your feelings and, besides, you looked good in it for me. You could have worn anything and looked good to me."

They were now nearing the bedroom.

"Victor," she called back over her shoulder, "if you expect me to behave as a good wife, and do the things you expect of me, you will have to tell me what you expect, and if you are going to do something that is illegal, tell me and I will protect you."

"Why, that's what all this conversation has been about, I thought."

"Then why not tell me the whole story and not this bit by bit way you have of talking to me."

From then on, he told it all and she faithfully recorded it. He knew now that he must change his tactics with her. He had an intelligent wife. He also knew the warning signal that when she called him Victor instead of Vic, she was upset. So the education of Roberta Lustig began.

TWO

VICTOR ADVISED HIS wife that he had some hasty business that would take him to Paris for a short time. He suggested she go to visit her mother in Kansas while he was gone. She expressed her disappointment. She wanted him to want her to be with him. He changed his mind immediately.

"You will go along, Bertie. But you must remember I cannot be with you much. My business will occupy me most of the time. But you can shop!" She was delighted at the thought of shopping in Paris. He told her that a student from the University would tutor her every morning for an hour in conversational French and German. He would try to be with her in the evenings, but there would be some evenings he could not. She accepted it all as business for him; what every man must do to earn a living. She told him she would study. He decided she wasn't going to be as difficult as he had thought.

The next morning he spoke to the men for whom he was doing business in Paris and asked them to pay the passageway and the expenses of two rather than one on this European trip. They agreed immediately. This 'Al Smith' must be a good honest man, he thought, judging by the willingness of his workers to go to any length for him. Politics wasn't so bad after all.

Van came to the hotel to see him about the double expenses. "How much will it cost you?" he asked Victor.

Victor pretended to think for a minute. Van was a man of wealth. Why shouldn't he be also?

"We too enjoy luxury," he replied after the moment of thinking. "We have our style of living and I can't ask my wife to give it up."

"Of course not, of course not," Van replied. "How much do you need?"

'Count' Victor Lustig gave him a sly grin. "Vud $5000 be all right?"

Funds were running low with Victor. The money his father had given him to finance his trip to America and, if he were careful, to last him a year, was almost exhausted. He must find some right away. This $5000 was a good beginning.

Victor had instructed Roberta that, when friends came to see him in their hotel, she should not leave immediately. She should stay and serve them a drink from their private well-stocked bar, and then retire to the bedroom. She had just served Van in the style of a perfect hostess and saw him reach in his pocket for the $5000.

'He didn't even have it in a wallet! It just seemed to be loose there, in his pocket. He took it out as though he were extracting a quarter,' she wrote. Then she added to the recording faithfully as she had begun. 'Will the time come when Vic will be as lavish in the use and spending of money? I am afraid it will.'

As Van left the room, he turned and came back, putting his arm on Victor's shoulder.

"Victor, why do you persist in this business of such dubious nature? I know I started it to befriend our governor, but you can stop at this very moment. Become an American citizen and I can assure you of one of the highest positions in the state of New York. You have the knowledge and the know-how to do it."

Just then, Victor Lustig had come to that 'convergence' in the road. He took the wrong road. If he ever regretted it in later years, he was too proud to come back and acknowledge his mistake. His only thought now was to clear the name of his friend 'Freddie'. It would be treason to give up now, when he saw he could help him. He knew 'Freddie' was a good man and, thanks to Van's influence, he vowed at the moment he took the 'wrong' road that he would never swindle a good man or a poor man. However, 'Count' Victor Lustig had another side. Money was an influence too.

After Van left, Roberta said to her husband, "You have some straw in your hair, Vic".

He reached up to brush his hair and his wife laughed. Roberta records the incident thus:

"He had never heard the expression and his feelings were hurt. I apologized and tried to explain what I meant, but I only seemed to make things worse. I'll never do anything like this to him again."

But many expressions of his she would not change, she wrote later in her diary. "I would never have wanted to change him, just enlighten him enough to protect him."

The incident helped Victor Lustig to grow up too. Never again would he let his personal feelings come between him and his beloved one – or a mark.

"You teach me and I'll teach you," he said to Roberta. "Teach me all the American slang and the jokes and the expressions."

But despite his willingness to learn from his wife, Victor Lustig was self-taught. He would listen to no one, even his best friends. He had declared his independence at the age of 12; when his father brought a violin down on his head in his frustration over his son's unwillingness to study it.

The well-to-do, dogmatic and proud father of two sons, Ludwig Lustig, had planned their careers. Victor would be a musician. He would be a great violinist. He saw music in him from the time he was a baby, old enough to stand up and beat time to the music around him. He would rival the greatest of the masters.

"Mein Viktor," he thought proudly, "he is my son and can be a great musician. I will give him every chance. As for Emil, the younger one, he is not my Viktor, but I will make something of him too."

When Victor was 12 years old his father said to him, "My son, I have bought you a very expensive violin. You are to take lessons from the greatest masters in all Austria. You will go to Vienna and live with relatives there and be close to your master for daily lessons of two hours."

Victor Lustig's rebellion began at that very moment. He would not go to Vienna for violin lessons. He ran away and went to Paris. There, for two months, he lived in various quarters without being detected as a runaway. He even found shelter in a house of prostitution, where the 'Madam' was kind to him and never once let him be harmed. Finally, the police found him and returned him to his father.

The elder Lustig was a wealthy merchant, dealing in pipes and tobacco, in Zurich and Prague. Of mixed German, Swiss and Czech descent, he had his principal business in Prague and his permanent home in Zurich. He was the burgomeister of Hostienne, Czechoslovakia, when Victor was born. He was used to dominating all 'scenes' in which he appeared. Now he was facing his 12 year-old son, who had run away and disgraced him.

When the police returned his son to him, they also returned a package. It lay on the table beside them. Victor knew what was in it. He eyed it now, slowly opened it and took out the precious violin. He carefully raised the instrument, pointing to the ceiling, and, with all the force of his more than average strength, every muscle in his large body taut, brought it down on the boy's head with a force that destroyed the violin.

That ended violin school for the boy, but he went to school in Dresden as his father later planned. Victor did enjoy learning; it was only the violin instructions that were blocked out of his mind forever. He himself acknowledged once in a letter he wrote from a prison cell. "I have never ceased going to school. I have a consuming thirst for knowledge and have always been able to find it, one way or another."

"Mein Viktor, I will give you one more chance," Ludwig Lustig told his son. "You will run my business. You can be a rich man."

So the Hostienne burgomeister sent this genius of a son to the expensive school in Dresden. There Victor learned languages; he knew six before he died and spoke German and French most fluently. Deep inside, however, Victor knew he would never be the business man his father wanted him to be. Not knowing what he would do, he began a life of traveling; of learning the ways of the world. He developed hobbies: dog races, horse races, sailing, gambling, billiards and chess. He mounted butterflies and became an expert at it. He loved birds and all animals. He loved music, especially the opera; he enjoyed reading, especially history and philosophy. He was a conversationalist on any subject. His genius mind seemed to be as broad as the world; if only he could find its niche in it.

Although refusing to study violin, he remained a music lover. In those days, before radio and television, he collected music boxes, clocks and watches. Wherever he was, all through his life, there must be music.

Ludwig Lustig never lost contact with this son. His dreams of greatness for him would not die. When Victor announced that he wanted to go to America, the loving father had a flicker of hope. In America he could have a fresh start; he could become the great person Ludwig dreamed for him. His father helped him to secure a passport and provided him with enough money to last a year, if he would be frugal and wise.

When Victor Lustig sat in the office of his friend Van and talked with the three politicians from New York, he showed interest in the plan. He wanted to vindicate his friend 'Freddie', who was being maligned by his political enemies. His slight acquaintance with Frederick Stuart Greene, highway commissioner of New York in 1919, amounted to a debt of infinite value, Lustig thought.

THREE

THIS TIME THEY were going to Europe as Mr. and Mrs. Eric Von Kessler. "Business and my work necessitates it," Victor told his wife. She made a mental note to find out if 'Von Kessler' was a family name of the Lustigs.

He told her that this was the last time they would travel together as man and wife. Victor was taking on a new 'profession' and it was better if he did not have a wife with him.

"But I can always flirt with you," he said with a chuckle, "and no one will know that you are my wife."

Since this was their last trip together as husband and wife, Roberta decided to do it right and didn't make a single mistake; she could have been born of royalty as far as the other passengers knew.

The Paris visit was nice but not long enough. Roberta visited the Eiffel Tower almost daily after her tutoring lessons. She loved it and promised herself if they would ever have children, which she hoped fervently, she would bring them here and tell them about it whenever they visited Paris.

She shopped daily and bought some beautiful evening gowns. One of them was her favorite, a green velvet evening gown with a cape. Victor was satisfied with the trip. He flirted with Roberta as he passed her on the deck and winked at her, not flirting with any other women. She watched him closely for that. Her jealousy was as great as his gaiety. Their round trip had been paid for and he had an excess of 15,000 American dollars on him, hidden in little secret pockets which his tailor, recommended by Van, had made for him. For the rest of his active life he wore such tailored suits with numerous hidden pockets, and he always kept them stocked with currency.

The day after his return he called Van, who scheduled a meeting with the three politicians. As they sat around the spacious office table in Van's office, Victor told them that he had made the proper contacts and was ready to help them, not because of his interest in politics or in Al Smith, whom he had never met, but because it would give him the opportunity to clear the name of his friend, 'Freddie'.

"How does it happen," one of the men interrupted him, "that you are so eager to clear the name of Frederick Greene, when you have only a slight acquaintance with him as you said?"

Victor knew that now was the time to tell 'Freddie's' story.

"Frederick Stuart Greene was in Paris during the war, he was a colonel in General Pershing's army. I was there too, a medical reject from the German army. One night I had two girls on my hands, both French; nice girls. A friend who was to go with me on this double date at the last minute could not keep his appointment, so, as I said, I had these two girls on my hands. Well, I ran into 'Freddie'. He was off duty that night and I asked him if he wouldn't like to join us. Someone had found a goose and the girls were going to cook it if the men would bring the drinks. 'Freddie' accepted my invitation. A night's entertainment would be a good change."

"After the goose dinner, we decided that dancing would be a good ending of the evening, so the four of us set out for the dance parlor. At the bottom of the stairs outside the girls' apartment, we ran into my girl's 'boyfriend'. He took one look at me with his girl and with a fist as big as my head, he knocked me flat."

"Here, in this public hall, the whole thing looked like a street brawl and the police were alerted at once. 'Freddie', who wasn't supposed to be there at all, risked his position in Pershing's army in this off-limits area. He literally pulled me out a back door before the police arrived. So you see why I want to do something for him. He saved me from arrest and probable incarceration at the risk of his own reputation. So, gentlemen, I am eternally grateful to him."

"You gentlemen are defending the reputation of the governor of New York and I am just as interested in clearing the name of his 'Director of Transportation.'"

The four politicians were delighted to see him interested in any way. They laid their plan after listening to Victor's suggestions. The men had decided Victor would obtain forged papers which, while illegal in themselves, would show how the 'Judge' was using illegal methods. An illegal reasoning to be sure, but all was legal in politics, especially during the early years of the 20th century.

Al Smith was a good, honest governor whose reforms could clean up government and politics in the state of New York; 'if' he had another term in office. Governor Smith was a social reformer. As governor, he improved conditions at state institutions and tried to improve the conditions of public administration. He worked for recreational areas, better housing conditions, better labor conditions and showed the ineffectuality of prohibition.

In doing this, he attacked the inefficiency of previous administrations. He accused his predecessors of allowing politics to affect their appointments, as in the case of the train accident. That accident, he said, would not have happened had there been effectual administration.

But the 'Judge' who wanted his position, who wanted to be governor of New York, began to use some of the same tactics and turned the tables on Smith. His special target was Frederick Stuart Greene, the Highway Commissioner, who was

Victor Lustig's friend, 'Freddie'. The 'Judge' claimed that Greene was ineffectual as Highway Commissioner and brought false accusations against many of Mr. Smith's appointees. Mr. Smith knew what was going on but didn't know what to do about it. It was for this reason that his political friends in Van's office made their plans with 'Count' Victor Lustig.

Lustig appeared eager to go ahead with their scheme. He had brought back with him from France forged papers that could discredit the 'Judge' in time if they could induce him to use them. That would be Lustig's job: to make the 'Judge' so want the papers that he would pay any price for them. 'Count' Victor Lustig had found his first mark in America.

At a dinner given that night for Lustig and his wife, they discussed the plans further. The four politicians told Lustig that there would be a dinner party in Washington given by a certain senator, who also had political aspirations. They told Victor and Roberta that they would be invited and that the 'Judge' would be there. That would be the time for Lustig to meet his mark, the 'Judge'.

They knew Senator George, who was giving the party. They also knew that this 'Senator' would grasp at any straw to improve his status. They telephoned him and told him that a certain 'Count' and 'Countess' Von Kessler were visiting in New York and asked him if he would like to invite them to his party. Would he?!? He would do anything to have royalty at his party.

"But my wife doesn't have an accent," Victor objected.

"Well then, she can be a rich American who snagged a 'Count'. That will be as good." So Victor and Roberta were invited to the party as 'Count and Countess Eric Von Kessler.' All expenses would be paid for their trip to Washington, of course. On the way back to the hotel, Vic had whispered to Roberta, "I am going to hire a maid and houseboy for us."

"Vic, that's silly. You have already promised me that we could have a home, an apartment. You know how much I want it."

"Well then, if that's what you want, an apartment we shall have. We'll look for a nice one before we go to Washington and select the furniture."

They found a satisfactory apartment and ordered furniture. Roberta hoped they would have time to live in it, but it could be home base anyway; a place they could always come to when they were free. The furniture was not yet delivered when they left, but Victor found a German maid who would live in the apartment and take care of the furniture when it arrived.

In Washington, they were met at the train station by the chauffeur of the Mayor of New York, Jimmie Walker, and were taken to their suite of rooms in an impressive hotel. Roberta was too tired to be impressed and went to bed. She knew her husband loved her, but she now realized his love for luxury and was afraid it might be his undoing. All she wanted was a little home, children, and her Victor at her side.

The next morning, they had breakfast in their rooms. Roberta announced that she would have her hair done in the salon and would prepare for the night's party.

The day would be long, but she would plan for it and do her best to please her husband. A call from his friends told him that all was in order for the party. The Mayor's chauffeur would call for them in his limousine, so that the 'Count' and 'Countess' could make their entrance at the proper time.

Before going to the beauty salon, Roberta made a purchase; a note book in which she could record everything that happened to her and Victor. It would be better than the scraps of paper upon which she had been making her recordings up to that time.

When she came back from the beauty salon after having her hair arranged by a master from London, she was so beautiful, her husband thought, that he walked around her and gazed upon her with admiration. Even so she wasn't impressed; she never realized her beauty. But she was so proud of what her husband said of her that she vowed to never not look beautiful for his sake. She had loved him when she married him, but now it was a form of adoration. That night she wore the green velvet Paris gown and her husband's admiration knew no bounds when she put it on. The gown had a floor-length cape, satin lined to match the gown, all adding to her elegance. What Roberta always remembered about the gown was the price she paid for it. She would never forget the price and told her daughter over and over about it, all her life. Victor placed a platinum and diamond bar pin at her bossom and a platinum watch with diamonds around her long white gloves. With her silk-like hair and her milk-white skin, she was divine as she stood before him.

The Mayor picked them up in a long limousine driven by a chauffeur. Victor squeezed Roberta's hand and told her that some day they would have their own limousine like this one, also driven by a chauffeur. She tried to tell him that it was not necessary. The Mayor, overhearing the conversation, said that the limousine was not his; it belonged to the city, but Victor insisted.

"Someday you will ride in ours." They did, three years later.

"My father always told me how beautiful my mother was that night," his daughter said many years later, "and as a child, it was my favorite story that I always wanted him to tell. 'Tell me about my beautiful mother in her green velvet dress!'" He never tired telling it. In later years, when her mother and father were separated, she would ask him to repeat the story, hoping that it would bring them together again; but it didn't work.

Senator George's exclamation, "My God, yes!" was hardly said when they were ushered in to his elaborate party. 'Countess' Von Kessler was well aware of the purpose of their attendance at this party and was willing to suffer along with anything her husband wished. Her suffering at the moment was the size four shoes into which she had pressed her 4½ size foot. Then, too, when Victor had laced her up to fit her into the green velvet dress, she thought that she would never breathe freely again, but she did. She was resplendent as they entered as 'Count and Countess'. It seemed that all eyes were upon her. But Victor's eyes were only for one person, the 'mark' whom he was to meet. Roberta was still not fully aware of the profession into which her husband was leading her. They could not be called rebels, but they would shame any younger generation with their bold and fantastic ventures, while still keeping the dignity of a lady and gentleman. There must be some other way one could repay another for a bad deed.

The meeting with the 'Judge' was brief. Victor wanted it that way – never any eagerness to meet and talk with his mark. In fact, he was disappointed with him. He was not impressive at all. Sort of a passive personality, but he soon found out his political ambitions.

That night Roberta made one of her monumental comments: "I wonder where he hung his bib overalls."

Roberta drifted off after they had met the 'Judge' and left Victor to visit with him. They discussed European politics and Voctor asked him politely a few questions about his own position. Casually, he said he had known Frederick Stuart Greene in Europe. He was disturbed to find now that he had been appointed Highway Commissioner. He stated how he detested the man and would do anything to destroy him.

He knew men in Europe, Lustig told the 'Judge', who would do anything to see him destroyed.

"How much would it cost?" the 'Judge' asked.

Lustig thought for a moment. "Oh, I would say about $25,000."

The 'Judge' was ripe for the picking by this time and Lustig excused himself; politely stating that he had enjoyed the conversation and hoped they could continue it sometime. When he walked Roberta in to dinner, she whispered, "Well?"

He answered under his breath, "Be quiet."

"My feet are killing me," Roberta answered.

Victor returned in a whisper, "Keep your shoes on or I will spank your bottom."

Thus they both covered up what was supreme to them at the moment. At the table, the 'Judge' was placed beside Roberta, Victor at her other side. The 'Judge' and Lustig entered into a conversation behind her back.

The 'Judge' said: "Count Von Kessler, the price is very high."

The 'Count' replied, "I know only the best and the purpose is success. I have no control over such people. They tell me how much and I pay it."

They attempted to talk later but the 'Count' said, "This is no place to discuss it. I'll see you after dinner in the library." But after dinner in the library was no place to discuss such matters the 'Count' decided, and told the 'Judge' that he would see him the next morning in the hotel.

The evening that followed was a successful and interesting one for 'Count' Victor Lustig. His wife, playing her part to the hilt despite shoes that were too small and a corset laced too tightly, was the cynosure of all eyes. He had disposed of his errand and had met many interesting people. They enjoyed discussing Europe and the future, the conditions following the war, which was no longer putting a damper on the very rich for traveling. He would act as adviser to many of them for their next visit to his countryland. The economy was a disaster, but all the countries needed tourism. Victor Lustig could help both the tourists and the countries they would tour.

The Mayor tired of the evening early and suggested that they go back to their hotel. Roberta kicked her shoes off in the limousine and could not get them back on again. The 'Countess' had to walk in stocking feet into the hotel.

FOUR

TIRED AS SHE was, Roberta recorded the whole evening's activities in her new notebook. All she really understood about the dinner party was that her husband knew some person whose job performances was excellent and the results of his work had saved the state millions of dollars. The governor had appointed the right man to the right job. That is what she recorded, adding that she didn't know why her husband was so interested in this man. Years later she added the correct details.

She went on to record that she felt sorry for Mrs. George, the wife of the senator who was giving the party. Her husband was so 'star-struck' that he made a fool of himself at the party. Mrs. George, she felt, was a nice woman, one whom she would like to have as a friend. With her husband's profession however, she wondered if she would ever have any friends. Victor announced that they would be going back to New York the next day, so she could not accept an invitation to have lunch with Mrs. George.

'Count' Victor Lustig met with the 'Judge' the next morning. They discussed what could be done to discredit at least one of the appointees of Governor Smith. The 'Judge' was impressed and satisfied that he was dealing with a very knowledgeable man regardless of his title, and agreed to pay $15,000. "If it can't be done for that, we will have to forget it," the 'Judge' said. Lustig wasn't so sure, he would do what he could; perhaps, since the war, forged papers were not so much in demand and 'they' might do it for less.

"You understand, of course," Lustig said to him, "that the papers you will receive will appear to be duplicates, for the originals must be filed with the Paris police and in Scotland Yard. This means double work, for the people who must place the files must be paid. Both Scotland Yard and the Paris police keep their files under lock and key, so it will be a difficult job to get these files placed. Those people who do the work for you must be well paid. Remember, they are forged papers, alleging crimes that never took place. You see how careful one must be. The offense must be authentic."

The 'Judge', still trying to cut costs, asked: "What is the purpose of placing these files in Scotland Yard and in the files of the Paris police? I don't understand this extra work. All I am asking for are forged complaints and copies of arrests of this man."

'Count' Victor Lustig looked dumbstruck. He sat back and gazed at the judge, registering both shock and disbelief. He opened his cigarette case, placed his cigarette in its silver holder, lit it and just sat there smoking. The 'Judge', watching him, seemed uncomfortable and finally said:

"I'm very sorry, sir. I must ask you again what you are talking about."

Now was the time for the 'diplomat' to begin. 'Never insult a mark.' You can insult him enough to make him pull out of the whole thing. Show him the errors of his ways, but be a 'diplomat'.

"I have spent little time in this country," Victor began slowly, "but I am sure of the fact that if you accuse someone, you must prove it. Is that not so here in America?"

"Of course. I am a lawyer and a judge. Certainly, that is our system and it is a good one."

"Then may I point out to you before we plan further, when you present the forged documents to the newspapers, do you sincerely believe they will not investigate before printing your accusations, knowing you are in politics? Do you think they will take them and print them immediately without any other proof? And then, could not the accused man ask for proof of the charges in the Paris police files, knowing there is nothing there because he was never in trouble with the law all the time he was in Paris?"

Lustig thought to himself about the time 'Freddie' had saved him after an innocent street brawl. He continued to the judge:

"And the Scotland Yard by this time will have heard of it and can check their files for proof to follow-up on the case. You would be in jeopardy, sir, and I would not be a part of it. The Paris police must be able to go to their files and locate the original complaint, the arrest, and the fine. This is not only to verify your accusations but to protect your good name."

By this time the 'Judge' was ready to declare the error of his ways. He said: "My God, I never looked at it from that angle. What's the matter with me? You are quite a man, Count. Now I understand the cost." He sat a moment in silence and finally said: "It's all worth it; it has to be done."

Victor and his wife left for New York the next day. He was eager to see the crusaders for Governor Smith and tell them that their plan would work.

He met with the politicians again and told them that the 'Judge' was dishonest and that he would go ahead with the plan. He would return to Paris, contact a forger whom he had found on his previous trip, and get forged papers of the highest quality. These the 'Judge' would present to the newspapers as false evidence against the governor and his highway commissioner. When the newspapers checked with the Paris police and found that they were false, the 'Judge' would be exposed, his political future ruined and Governor Smith and Frederick Greene vindicated.

The plan, of course, necessitated another trip to Paris. Roberta this time said she would sooner not go. Their furniture had arrived and she wanted to remain to make the apartment into a home for them.

Victor had planned with the judge, after a $5,000 advance payment, to notify him from Paris how much it would cost him. When he reached Paris, he found that the forger he had contacted did not show up. He mentally decided he was not the man he wanted if he was an indecisive man. He would find someone else. His passport read 'Eric Von Kessler'. He used German names as a rule when he traveled under an alias because of his flawless German. He contacted an old school friend in Paris, 'Peter', and told him of his dilemma.

Peter pleaded with his old friend, "Victor, why do you waste your time? You are brilliant and appear to be a man of wealth. Why don't you go into business and do things that are legal?"

"Peter," Victor responded, "I would go mad behind a desk. This way I am free, rich, and happy."

Peter told him of a man, not living in Paris but in Rheims; a baker. Victor went to Rheims to contact this 'baker'. He found 'Claude' working 12 hours a day for a meager salary. He could not afford to take any time off, he said, so it would take several weeks to produce the kind of papers 'Von Kessler' wanted. But he could do it, was glad to do it, and needed the money. He added that his work was considered flawless.

Victor told him that he must have the papers quickly and he must wait in Rheims for them. The baker said that for enough money, he could afford to be sick and not appear at work for four days and could possibly complete the work the Americans wanted.

'Claude' said he had the various kinds of paper and parchment used in each country and the respective seals. Victor thought he would not need any seals, just papers from the French police incriminating the man who had been General Pershing's aide while he was in Paris. The baker told him he could do it and showed him two boxes, one containing various discs about the size of a silver dollar and another containing the holder for these discs. Victor seemed pleased with the possibilities and offered him more than his usual charge, telling him he might be using his services again in the future.

That's how Victor always got things done. You get what you pay for, he would say. He wrote to the 'Judge' and told him it would require more money immediately and advised him to send it to his Paris address, which was that of his friend, 'Peter'. He was certain the 'Judge' would write enough in the letter to incriminate himself and that would be further evidence to put in the hands of the 'friends' of Governor Smith.

Finally, 'Claude' told him that he was ready and presented him with the finest set of forged papers he had ever seen. Victor then decided that this baker should own his own bakery, hire someone to run it in the mornings and go into business with him. 'Claude' and Victor Lustig were then in business together. They remained in business together until 1931.

Victor then departed for Paris to await the reply of the 'Judge'. The latter included an additional $10,000 and a note that said: "Please return as soon as possible. I can use this 'paper work' you have and need it immediately."

Lustig pocketed the $10,000 and returned to New York at once. He also won several thousand dollars on the return trip playing cards with wealthy Americans aboard, who seemed delighted to lose their money.

When he returned to New York, Roberta met him poutingly.

"Vic, I don't like this sort of life. You can't leave me alone again. I want to go with you wherever you go."

"Why, you can, Buckle, of course."

"...and I promise, Vic, I won't be a drain on you. I can help you if you let me."

"Of course, Buckle, of course, you shall go along with me."

She snuggled up to him. "I thought, Vic, I was going to have some news for you when you got back. But I was wrong. There's not going to be a baby."

"That's good, Buckle, it will be better to have a child when we are more settled."

"That's a laugh," Roberta said somewhat sadly, "Will we ever be settled?"

Victor didn't answer. He didn't tell her how right she was, how unsettled she would always be as the wife of 'Count' Victor Lustig.

After the politicians had carefully photographed the forged documents and kept copies of them all, including the letter; Victor departed to meet the 'Judge' and deliver the forged documents to him. He was bored with the whole thing by this time. He was tired and wanted to get it over with as soon as possible. He lost no time in showing the papers to the judge, who felt the paper and congratulated him for his good work. It took him over an hour to read the documents and look at the pictures Victor had produced through the efforts of Van and his friends. One of them even indicated prison pictures. All were reports of suspicions and arrests of 'Freddie' in Paris. The 'Judge' opened a leather case, removed an envelope and handed it to Lustig. It was the additional $10,000. Victor Lustig's total profit after payment from Van and his friends, which included expenses, was $35,000

The documents he was in such a rush for were not used for many months, not until the next campaign. They met with moderate success, but eventually were exposed and ruined the political future of the grasping 'Judge'.

Victor went immediately to his wife.

"Buckle, we are going to take a trip. We'll go to Kansas to see your family. Paul (Roberta's brother-in-law) has promised to take me fishing!"

Roberta was happy. She would see her mother again. After a few days' rest they were off in their first car for a trip to Kansas. Victor was happy too. His first mark in America had been as gullible as he expected and his work was assured for the future.

FIVE

ORGED PAPERS WOULD not be the only resource of Victor Lustig's new profession. As soon as business looked good in America, he designed a money box; a box that would attract greedy marks who were in trouble financially. He had heard once about a man from Germany who sold such a box to a wealthy man in England in 1890. That was the year Victor was born. But the money box that this German, Victor Lustig, sold to many marks, once for $102,000, was his own design. He found a man who would make them for him, usually five or six at a time, according to the original pattern Victor had given him.

He always used rose wood or cedar for the box, constructed with brass trim and encased in a leather carrier. Inside was a system of rollers that would crank out bills that were put in it, along with blank paper on which the money box, by using a certain chemical, was supposed to imprint new bills. When the duped buyer found that the blank paper which he had fed into the machine still came out blank pieces of paper, Victor Lustig would have allowed enough time to be cities away. He would tell the buyer that it would take 12, 18 or 24 hours for the chemical to work and the machine to crank out bills for them according to the time he estimated it would take him and his chauffeur, always waiting with a car ready to go, to be away to some unknown destination. Because the person buying the money box was dishonest and was a crook himself -he only sold it to persons who, after careful research, proved to be dishonest- he could not cry 'catch that crook' and the maker of the machine felt secure from repercussions.

Victor Lustig had an ingenious method of providing clean or legitimate money for the first cranking. Every purchaser of the money machine at the first cranking got legitimate bills, which the buyer thought of course were counterfeit, but which could always be cashed at a bank. 'Count' Lustig would assure this to the buyer when he made a sale.

He would obtain new $100 bills in sequence of nine from a bank. He would go to a bank in the New York area and some other banks in major cities, where he had made arrangements, with $50,000 in legitimate money and obtain newly minted

$100 bills not only in the sequence of nine but also in sequence of six. He would leave with $45,000 in $100 bills, $5,000 having been left with the bank teller who did the work for him. At home or in a locked hotel room, equipped with a razor blade, a bright light, a special ink and pen, egg white, white gloves and a green visor; he would set to work changing the numbers on each sequence.

Leaving the first sequential number ending in one, he carefully scraped with the blade the end numbers on the other eight bills and made them all end in one, three, or nine, so that all nine bills in each sequence would have the same numbers. This was the come-on legitimate money to point out to his 'customer' the perfection of his counterfeit bills. His daughter remembers, when she was a child, seeing him sitting late at night, working with money, wearing a green visor and the white gloves.

He used the egg white to put a glaze on the number, that had been removed and replaced with a new number, so that it did not show on the newly minted bills.

He always set the money box up with five or eight clean bills, 'legitimate money' that would come out when one $100 bill was inserted at the first cranking after the designated number of hours had expired. This was his demonstration; his sales pitch. Because all the numbers on the five or nine bills were the same after Lustig's doctoring had taken place, the buyer thought that they were counterfeit bills which the money box made and which Lustig assured them they could cash at any bank; for bank tellers never took time to look at numbers. But he would caution them not to cash more than one bill at the time at the same window to be safe.

To prepare the money box for selling, he would put the bills on a roller and roll them very carefully, bills end to end. The actual money inserted went into the top of the box and the pieces of blank paper, which were to be made into bills, would go on a roller at the bottom. All the time he was inserting the blank pieces of paper he would be explaining to the potential buyer how the machine worked, that a trap on the inside, after the designated number of hours, which was very important, would roll the counterfeit bills to the top and they would come out backwards. Thus every buyer had $900 or $600 clean money out of the machine, but for which he had paid dearly.

It was expected that a percentage of the buyers would get impatient and cut the time allotted him to make new bills and turn the crank in 11 or less hours but, after the first time, no money would come out. He would, of course, think that his failure to wait the designated number of hours was the cause. When he would finally realize that, no matter how many hours he waited, no money came out; if he should want to find the 'foreign' man who had sold him the box, he wouldn't know where to find him.

Once, by accident, a victim of the money box saw Lustig on the street in Chicago. He started after him. Lustig, always a poor driver, in his haste to avoid his pursurer, hit an iron post. He jumped out of his car and began running. The pursurer caught him and surprised Lustig by calling out only:

"I've done something terrible – something terrible!"

"What did you do?"

"I think I have hurt my machine. Help me."

"Well, what?"

"I didn't wait the 12 hours you told me to wait. I turned the crank in 11 hours and money came out. I put the blank paper you gave me in, put in two drops of the solution just as you told me, and this time waited only 10 hours. Only blank paper came out. I tried the full time after that and still only blank paper came out. I must have damaged the machine."

"Yes, you have destroyed the machine," Lustig told him. "I told you to wait 12 hours. What did you expect?"

"I want another machine."

"Why you fool, you have destroyed the machine. You'll have to pay me $25,000 for another machine."

The duped man left after some argument, full of guilt that he had destroyed the magic box he had bought. Lustig never heard from him again as he probably could not produce $25,000 for another machine and couldn't have found 'Count' Victor Lustig anyway.

Jubilant over the success of his first venture in America, that with the politicians, the "Judge' and the success of his money box, Victor Lustig started out to look for other marks. He was making new friends daily, friends whom he trusted and respected and whom he would never think of swindling, but he was also making friends among another element of political, economic, and social America whom he settled upon at once as potential marks. He figured that bankers would make good marks. They had access to lots of money and they were often tempted to use the bank's money for their own schemes with the intention of putting it back before the auditors came around.

He soon heard of one such a banker, George Harrison, an honest man whom temptation had felled.

But before he could pursue this new banker mark, Victor found that he had a problem, one that might prove serious if he did not handle it prudently.

'Philipi', his chauffeur, was dishonest. Victor found that he was taking money from him regularly. Decoys of $100 left around soon proved his suspicions. He was afraid to fire him, for he feared that he knew too much as he had driven him on his many trips and he would talk. It could ruin him. He telephoned a friend in Florida to help him out.

Roberta had announced good news to him shortly before this. They were going to have a baby and she wanted the baby to be born in California. She had driven out there, with a stop in Kansas to announce the good news and take Mamma along with her. Their furniture had been shipped out and she was at home there waiting for her baby. It would be a little girl, the father-to-be insisted and bought everything in pink. He filled the baby's room with toys, dresses, booties, beautiful little coats and bonnets, all pink. The crib, high chair, pottie chair, cabinet and dresser had wide, pink satin ribbon woven through the tubular openings around the sides of the bed.

Roberta laughed a lot, and grandmother, servants, and friends teased Victor: "What if it's a boy?"

He would stand his ground and say, "No, she von't. We shall have a little girl."

Roberta and her mother were now settled in their new home with all the lovely furniture. Victor had been nervous about her trip alone and had kept in touch with her all the way.

"Now that we'll have another mouth to feed, I'll have to be busy making more money." He was determined that his child would be born, not with a silver spoon in her mouth, but with a diamond-studded one!

On his last trip with 'Philipi' as chauffeur, he had a package to mail to his wife. Ordinarily, he would have sent 'Philipi' into the post office to mail the package, but now, as he looked down and saw Roberta's address on the package, he realized that it would be too dangerous for his chauffeur to know his wife's address, so he went into the post office himself to mail the package. He was ready to leave and turned around to see a picture of himself as 'WANTED' glaring at him. Members of the FBI were already looking for him and he had not realized it. He got out of the post office as quickly as possible and realized more than ever that he must get rid of 'Philipi', but in a way that there would be no reprisals. He dared not fire him, for 'Philipi' knew too much to let him leave under any shadow. That is when he appealed to his friend in Florida.

"I am sending 'Philipi' on vacation in Florida. Make him an attractive offer down there that he will want to accept. Don't let him return, whatever you do."

The friend responded, offered 'Philipi' a big job as caretaker of a large estate, which the dishonest chauffeur accepted, and resigned his job as Victor Lustig's chauffeur.

Now he would return to his latest mark 'to make enough money to feed that extra mouth' that would be in the family.

SIX

LUSTIG WAS READY to get back to his banker and his marks. Charlie McCord, his English friend, was his helper this time. George Harrison, the banker, whom he first spotted as a mark, was a brilliant speculator, but he had over-speculated, over-extended and over-spent. He originally was an honest man in every respect. He had brought many people to wealth by his investments, which he was always happy to make for his clients. He had known Charlie McCord for years and through him had met Victor and Roberta. He liked them, despite knowing from Charlie what Victor did. Now that he was in trouble and did not know where to go, he asked Charlie about Victor. He wondered what could be done. He had gone out on a limb and invested money from an estate without any signatures. Now the limb was slipping and his wife caught him staring at his gun. She was frantic and called Charlie. He was willing to try at least.

When Charlie presented the case to Lustig, the latter realized that Harrison was essentially honest and decided to help him. He outlined this plan to Charlie. There were two German self-called financiers in this country who wanted to invest their money in American banks. He would induce them to invest in Harrison's bank. Charlie and Victor made their plans. They would meet at Grant's Tomb. That would be an interesting meeting place. Grant, Lustig knew, had been involved in a fraudulent banking scheme after his presidency. So what more appropriate place to meet? There was also a restaurant close by, a German restaurant, where they could hold their meeting. The three men arrived simultaneously but the Germans had not yet arrived. Suddenly, they saw the two men walking toward the tomb some 20 blocks from their hotel.

"My God, who's being taken?" Charlie cried out. "We're talking about $200,000 and they walk 20 blocks to save taxi fare?"

They all five crowded into a cab and directed the driver to take them to the German restaurant. They were all tired, Victor from his trying episode with 'Philipi', Harrison from his worry over the bank situation, Charlie from the excitement of the whole thing, and the two German marks, supposedly from their 20-block walk.

They ordered their dinner in silence. The Germans knew the German menu, so there was no trouble in ordering. Victor was so tired by this time that he didn't care whether the thing went through or not. Charlie said afterward that the only reason he did go through with the deal was poor George Harrison in the fix he was in.

By the time dinner was over, they had convinced the two Germans, Heinrich Stahlecker and Ernst Rascher, that they could invest $150,000 in notes and $50,000 that German friends were interested in investing in Harrison's bank. Just then two FBI men strolled in and sat down at a table close by. The owner warned Victor who they were. Charlie paid the tab and they prepared to leave, after setting up a meeting for Monday morning at the bank. There they would see Harrison seated behind the desk of a famous bank and be impressed.

They took a cab, the five of them, dropped Stahlecker and Rascher off at their second-rate hotel, dropped a very nervous Harrison off by his own car and retired to their hotel.

Lustig had an idea. He was observing the marks closely and, from all indications, they were not honest. They had said they walked 20 blocks to Grant's tomb and he was sure they didn't. They were lodged in the poorest hotel in that area. They could not be the rich German financiers with money to invest that they pretended to be.

"Maybe we had better drop the whole thing," Charlie suggested.

"Not on your life," Victor responded.

"What are you going to do, 'Count' Lustig?"

"I am going to outsmart a fox," Victor answered with a wicked grin. "I am going to pay a visit to one of these gentlemen tomorrow morning and you are coming with me. You will drive me there, since I have no chauffeur and you will wait at the madam's across the street from their hotel."

Charlie jumped out of his seat, "Not me, old boy, not me!"

But 'Count' Lustig the next morning had Charlie drive him to the hotel where the German marks were staying, store the car in a nearby warehouse, and wait at the madam's, where he had convinced Charlie he would have to endure no further activity except waiting.

"There is not a better place to find a mark than at a madam's," Victor told him. "Make acquaintance with the madam, but don't enter any of their business. They are the best people in the world to point out a mark to you. They know them all." Was he remembering his days under the protection of a madam?

Lustig took out of the car a leather bag, polished like the boots of a general, and, carrying it into the hotel, knocked on the door of Ernst Rascher.

"What have you there, my friend?" Rascher inquired, looking curiously at the exquisite case that Lustig carried.

"I have a very unusual and unique American tool that I might show you if you will promise not to tell your friend next door."

He sat down, placing the leather case at his feet, his walking stick balanced against the bed and his hat on his knee. Rascher was becoming more interested and curious.

"May I see this mysterious object?"

"Not yet, sir, until you tell me what is your secret visit other than my visit with you, Mr. Harrison, and Mr. McCord."

Then Rascher became suspicious. "You are police?" he blurted out.

"I must confess, my friend," Lustig said, "that I am associated with the police. I have decided your friend is not of the quality that I see in you, so I decided to talk with you first. I will not tell my superior until I have talked with you and heard your story. Then I will decide whether I should turn you in or not. And, my friend, I must remind you that I must have the truth right or I will be obliged to use that against you."

By now Rascher was in panic. "What can I do to straighten things out with you? Tell me and I will do it."

After about 20 minutes of letting himself be persuaded, 'Count' Lustig said, "All right, I do not want your friend Stahlecker or my friend Harrison to know that I work with the police. If you will assist me in capturing these people in illegal acts, I will speak for you and see that you are released if the police get you."

After considerably more negotiations, the two seemed to have arrived at a meeting point and Rascher ventured timidly: "Could I still see the object you have there?"

The 'Count' considered. "Well, since you are such a good fellow and plan to cooperate, I will share with you a secret. This is a money box which I discovered on a man for whom I searched for a long time and whom I finally caught. The box makes counterfeit money. Here, I'll show you."

Lustig pulled a crisp $100 bill from his pocket, inserted the bill in a slot of the machine as he explained it was about time, twelve hours had passed and the machine was due to pay off and he turned a crank and watched six $100 bills slowly emerge from the box, five new ones and the original he had put in.

Rascher, eyes protruding, face nearly blue, backed up against the bed to sit down, stumbled over the walking stick, frantically motioning toward the door of Stahlacher's room, finger over his tight, thin lips, cautioning his visitor to be quiet. He finally relaxed his tense body and turned to look again at the wonderful machine.

"I decided last night not to go along with Stahlecker and Harrison," he said as though feeling his way. "I'll have nothing to do with it. I haven't told them yet, but my mind is made up. Believe me."

He stroked the case of the magic box and suggested that they go elsewhere to discuss it. With the box returned to its elegant case, they retired to a quiet, secluded place in the lobby. Lustig excused himself and said he had to make a phone call. He called Charlie over at the madam's place.

"He swallowed the hook, I'll call you later."

Rascher greeted him with, "I'll cooperate with you if you'll cooperate with me."

"You forget, my friend, that I am a man of the law and cannot enter into any illegal deal. If you want the money box, I will consider selling it to you for a great amount of money."

They went to a nearby restaurant where there were few clients and they could talk privately.

"How much?" Rascher pleaded.

"No less than $100,000," 'Count' Lustig answered

"Impossible," the German cried. "I will have to leave you and go back to my own country. I have done nothing wrong."

He made a last effort. Looking Lustig squarely in the face, he asked, "Would you like to be very wealthy? I have a plan that would make us both wealthy, if you'll just cooperate."

Lustig looked at him, feigning surprise. "You forget, I am a man of the law and you are asking me to do something illegal? I can turn you in in a moment."

He looked Rascher squarely in the face and said "$75,000 for the money box. Not a dollar less."

Victor waited a few minutes, motioned the waiter for the check, placed his napkin on the table and prepared to leave. Rascher extended his hand.

"Yes, I'll buy the money box. It's a deal."

They agreed he would have the money Monday morning, sit in at the bank appointment in which he would have no part, deliver the money to Lustig and Lustig in turn would deliver the money box to him.

Lustig called Charlie again, and inquired laughing, "Did you enjoy yourself?"

"It wasn't as bad as I expected," Charlie answered him. "In fact the madam wasn't there and the maid served me a good breakfast."

"As I said before, you couldn't find a better place to locate a mark," Lustig told him. "They keep me alerted on them."

At the meeting at the bank on Monday morning, Harrison arrived first, then Charlie and Victor. Victor had time to tell Harrison briefly that Rascher was buying the money box and was backing out of any part with the banker. Stahlacker and Rascher arrived. Rascher showed that he was not interested but Stahlacker was all the more interested. When Rascher finally got up and said that he was having no part in the deal, Stahlacker said:

"My friend has not much patience, but I will buy his part too, if I can see some friends first."

"Not at all," Harrison exclaimed. "Now or not at all."

"Well then if you'll reduce by 2000 American dollars, I shall buy both parts." George accepted and the group broke up. Charlie to go his way, for good. He was an honest man and did not like what Victor was doing, nor Harrison either.

Harrison paid off his bank loan and soon retired from the bank. Victor exchanged the leather case he was guarding carefully all during the conference with Rascher for $75,000 with the words:

"You'd better get out of town fast, before the police catch up with you. Remember, I am a man of the law." Rascher left, running.

Victor turned to another important duty: to replace 'Philipi', his chauffeur. He must have someone whom he could trust, not only an honest person but one discreet enough to take him on his many 'business' trips and not ask why. He telephoned Tom Kearney, his good friend in St. Louis, and told him what he wanted. Tom's reply came immediately.

"I've got the man you want, Vic."

Victor answered, "When can he begin work?"

"Right now," came the answer. "And he can pay his way to New York. He'll be there tomorrow."

Tony came and Victor knew he had the man he wanted. He was a fine looking Italian with no family connections. Tony made the ideal chauffeur. He stayed with him for many years until illness caused his retirement to a milder climate, where Victor set him up in a successful restaurant business, and where Tony found a good wife and lived a long enough life after Victor's death to relate much of his master's life, as he experienced it, to Vic's former wife, Roberta, and Victor's daughter, Betty.

Tony never asked questions. He became a trusted intermediary and was there always when Lustig was ready to depart, much of the time in haste, with the simple question: "Where to, sir?" and wait to be told.

Now Victor must find a maid for his wife waiting out her pregnancy in California. He and Tony went to Detroit. He told Tony what he wanted, a good maid for his wife. Tony, in a short time responded that he had found someone. He had friends in Detroit and he appealed to them for help. They recommended one and Tony brought Ruby to his 'master's' room in the hotel. Ruby said she was willing to take the job and go to California to take care of his wife. She was hired on the spot. Victor liked Ruby immediately, but he didn't like her name. "I'd like to change your name to 'Grace'," he told her. She agreed and Grace it was from then on.

"I'd like to go shopping for my wife and baby," he told Tony and Grace. "Come and help me pick out some clothes." Tony drove them to a department store. Victor said he wanted Tony to help him buy some coats and suits for himself and Grace to try on dresses that his wife might like. When they left the department store, they packed box after box into their automobile, already filled with luggage of the three travelers. Out on the highway they stopped.

"We're going to have to make more room here. Tony, put on that heavy overcoat and throw the box away. Grace, off with your coat and put on the coat in that box. Then we can throw another box away. At our first stop, Grace, you can put on one of the dresses from one of the other boxes. Transfer the rest of the clothing into your suitcases and throw the boxes away." Gradually, Tony and Ruby, now Grace, realized that they had been choosing clothing for themselves in the department stores of Detroit.

When all the changes were made, Tony asked the usual question:

"Where to, sir?"

"Please don't call me sir," Victor said. "You may call me Victor. Now, get out your map Tony. We are going home, the best way you can find."

"But where is home, sir, I mean Victor."

"Home is California. I am going to be the father of a little girl."

The three were off to California with nothing to stop them except Grace's color.

"It won't rub off," Victor would assure the protestors, "and if it did it might improve your looks." A few bills, slipped into the hands of the doormen usually settled matters. But it took many tips to get Grace to California.

Thus Tony, Grace, and Victor Lustig drove in his Rolls Royce through the snow and sleet of the Midwest to California to celebrate the pending birth of a baby girl. It was winter, 1921.

SEVEN

Victor Lustig took his new-born daughter in his arms, pressed a wisp of a kiss on her forehead and laid her gently in the pink-ribboned crib. All had happened as he had planned. With Tony and Grace, he had arrived in time for Christmas and did not leave until the girl he had ordered, was born February 13, 1922. For fear of blackmail or kidnapping, Lustig rarely revealed he had a wife and daughter, but he loved them dearly and spent as much time with them as he could. The red headed girl that writers had him fleeing across country with was his wife. Wherever he went, they went along, shipping the furniture which, Roberta always insisted, helped to make the home she longed for.

This daughter was her father's darling. Most men want a son to hand down their name as well as their profession. Not so with Victor Lustig. He would not hand down his profession to anyone, but he would love a little daughter. "So it must be a girl," he told his wife as he bade her goodbye on her way to California. And after she came according to order, he loved her, was always proud of her. When he did not always acknowledge his wife and daughter publicly, it was not that he was ashamed of them, it was to protect them.

He gave his little daughter a long list of lovely names and had them all registered in Germany, but his favorite name for her was Skeezix, after the comic book character.

"I believe that was why I was always so close to my father," his daughter said in later years. "It was because he wanted me. I loved my father and my mother both. They told me that I never cried when they held me. But I felt most loved when my father said, 'My little Skeezix'. He was a tender man in many ways."

Betty Jean was taught from an early age never to talk about her father. If someone asked where he was, she was always to say, "I don't know." And she usually didn't know. Because their lives were always in danger, Roberta and little 'Skeezix' always had a body guard with them, either Tony or Grace.

Victor's many friends were still trying to persuade him to give up his illegal, precarious business. Tom Kearney in St. Louis never stopped talking to him about it. Van in New York had already offered him a high public office if he would change. Walter Winchell and Lionel Moise both pleaded with him to get out of the racket. Lionel, bitter at first over Roberta's blatant rejection that night she met Victor at the party in Kansas City, had become their friend. A New York banker spent hours pointing out the advantages of working for him at a top salary, and Roberta kept saying, "Please, Vic, give it a try."

Tom Mix and Rudy Valentino knew him and tried in vain to persuade him to give it all up. Tom was walking with him one day on Tom's ranch and said suddenly:

"You can ride horses, Vic. I could make a real cowboy out of you in the movies. Give it all up and try acting."

"No use, Tom. My acting pays better than yours. And the only horses I am interested in are those on the race track."

Walter Winchell said to him: "You are an intelligent man, Vic. You could study, take the tests and become an American citizen. Then you could teach languages, history, many things. You have a knowledge that is wasted."

Victor's answer was always: "I would be bored to death behind a desk. I could never do it."

It was true, dollar-wise, but in the long run, he found out later, too late, it might have been a good idea after all.

Many of these friends were news reporters, like Winchell and Moise. They, at any time, could have made a good story out of Victor Lustig's wife and daughter, shown their pictures, and revealed the fact that they existed. But none of them ever did. They had dinner with them in any home that Roberta was able to make as they moved from place to place. They enjoyed genial conversation and felt safe with them. But the Lustig family, with wealth greater than that of any of their friends, continued to be on the run.

In the life which he chose 'to be forever on the run,' Victor Lustig traveled under many aliases. 'Von Kessler' was his favorite alias and he was 'Count Von Kessler' more often than he was 'Count' Lustig. He also was known as C.H. Baxter, Rudolph Habegger, Victor Gross, Frank Gardner, Hermann Keller, Helmut Strode and once he was successfully Monsieur Andre Dupre and Pierre Duval. He died in prison as Robert V. Miller. All of this was to protect his wife and daughter more than himself. And he also loved the thrill of fooling the public, hiding behind a name facade.

John Barrymore taught him the art of make-up. Lustig always counted actors and movie stars among his friends. The actor in himself made him feel akin to them, although he would not join them in their profession. Rudolph Valentino, Marion Davies, Sophie Tucker, Fanny Brice counted him among their friends. Sophie Tucker and Roberta went to the races together whenever they could, though never without Victor.

Once when Victor and Roberta were attending a play in which John Barrymore performed, he went back stage after the performance. Nicky Arnstein and his wife, Fanny Brice, were with them, so he asked them to take Roberta to the night club where a party was planned following the performance. He would join them later. Back stage Barrymore was removing his make-up. Playfully Victor picked up the beard he was removing and put it on. John rose to the occasion and proceeded to make him up, bushy eye brows, side burns and all, all the time talking about the art of make-up.

Lustig wore the disguise to the party. No one recognized him. He walked past Roberta twice before she said, "Vic, is that you?" From that time on he used disguises of many forms to elude the law. He became a Jewish rabbi, a priest, a clown (he had many friends in the circus business), a bellhop, a waiter, a porter and a baggage man. Whatever disguise would suit the occasion, he would use it. They had 12 trunks, many of them filled with his theatrical make-up and disguises, which traveled with them wherever they went.

Once he was in a hat store, where a rabbi was buying a hat. Victor saw his old hat in his hand and offered to buy it. The rabbi wondered why any one would want his old hat, which was too old for him to wear, but he sold it at a nice little sum. A beard and a long black coat completed the outfit which he used many times. Once, when Secret Service agents were looking for him, he put on the rabbi garb. It was a Jewish holiday and the people were celebrating. He went out and mingled with the celebrating crowds. His wife, in her diary, even thought that he went into the Synagogue and read from the Talmud. The Secret Service lost him completely.

To be a priest, he needed only a black suit, a Roman collar and a black hat. Once a priest's long cassock disguised him and enabled him to make an escape when he knew the police were close on his track.

He was a clown at children's parties. These parties were always for the children of underworld men, notorious like himself, hunted men, who had families but could never stay in one place long enough for their children to make friends. These children lived lonely lives, as he knew his daughter did. He tried whenever he could to make up for this by throwing a big party and performing as a clown. His daughter remembers one party in particular. There were about 30 children present. The clown was the whole afternoon's entertainment. He performed all the antics the actor in him could conjure up, he showed his puppets, performed magic tricks and used his power as a ventriloquist. He treated them with candy, and pop corn. He had a one-man circus on a beach at a house he had rented in Florida.

Many years later, Roberta and a friend were shopping in Kansas City. Near Walnut and Main they saw a blind man and his tin cup squatted on the street close to them. Roberta stopped, struggled with her armful of packages to get to her purse, and drew out two large bills, which she deposited, not in the beggar's tin cup but in his hand, telling him what they were. They went on, the friend saying as they crossed the street, "Are you crazy, Bertie, giving that beggar all that money?"

"No, I'm not crazy, just grateful," Roberta replied. "One of them saved Victor from arrest years ago and I shall always be eternally grateful."

"Did I ever tell you, Bena, about Victor and the tin cup?"

"No," Bena replied, "but nothing you and Vic ever did would surprise me."

"It was one of those times when the FBI were making a nation-wide search for Vic. He was to meet his brother Emil at a cigar stand, which was a bookie. In the meantime, Emil went into a saloon for a drink and said with great importance upon leaving, 'I'm going to meet my brother, 'Count' (with great emphasis on the 'Count') Victor Lustig.'"

"The waiter who had served the drink happened to be an undercover FBI man. He immediately began trailing Emil. Tony, there with Emil, got the message and got to Victor in time to warn him that the FBI would probably meet him at the cigar stand. Vic looked around to see what to do. He spied a blind man, with a tin cup and pencils, not far from him and his ingenuity, always working over-time, was ready. Before the blind man realized what was happening, he was hustled into a Rolls Royce Vic was using then. The touch of a $100 bill in his hand assured the man that what was happening to him was good for him (though he had to take their word for the denomination). Soon, he had changed clothes with Vic and was riding away smiling from ear to ear in the Rolls Royce, minus his glasses, clutching a silver-handled walking stick and wearing slightly tight shoes. And on the street, they left behind a new 'blind man' with glasses covering bright eyes, in ragged clothes and with a hat pulled down over a seemingly weary face. He clutched a tin-cup filled with pencils and cried out weakly as shoes passed him by saying, "Help a poor blind man, sir. Buy a pencil."

"His profit in 30 minutes was 35 cents, 'a pretty good profit for doing nothing,' he chuckled to himself as he watched a fat lady drop a nickle in his tin and take three pencils. Suddenly, polished shoes appeared. FBI. Victor's heart almost stopped. The man seemed to pause. Finally, he dropped a dime into the tin cup but he did not take a pencil. Lustig could see from his stooped, head-lowered position that the 'polished shoes' moved to the side and stood there. He bought a paper, glanced through it, and seemed to stand aimlessly for awhile.

"Then the 'blind man' saw a cab draw up in front of the cigar stand. Emil stepped out and started paying the driver. 'Fool' Victor said to himself. 'Pay the cabbie while inside and disappear the minute you are out.'"

"'Polished shoes' began to move on toward the cigar stand. The crowd was moving in around the blind man. He would chance it now and get lost in the crowd. So he rose furtively and, leaving his tin box and pencils on the street, disappeared around a corner. He had transferred money to his ragged pockets, but no cab would stop for this beggar, so he boarded a street car and rode safely to his hotel. He entered by the garbage cans, used the service elevator to his room, and changed clothes. He packed and checked out. It was just as well that Emil didn't know where he was."

"My poor Vic," Roberta ended her story with a sigh. "He always wore a disguise. He could never be himself."

Bena pressed her arm silently as they crossed the street.

EIGHT

O LIN STARKEY WAS a produce king of Chicago. Or so he thought of himself. His produce wagons combed the city of Chicago, selling potatoes and other produce which farmers brought him every morning. Buying at a pittance and selling at a 100 percent profit made him the king of hucksters. Loud mouthed, crude and boastful, he oversaw the departure of his produce wagons every morning and exacted a complete accounting when they came back in the evening.

Victor's chauffeur, Tony, had a cousin in Chicago who knew Olin. Soft spoken and quiet, the exact opposite of Olin, Bennie, Tony's cousin, had no dealings with the 'King' but for some unexplainable reason they were both courting the same girl. Victor always saw to it that Tony had time to visit his friends when they were in cities in which any resided. Victor and his wife and daughter were staying at the Drake on Lake Shore Drive with Tony quartered in a room not far from them. One day Victor gave Tony a free afternoon and told him to go see his friends.

Tony happened along at the moment that the rivalry between the two men who were courting the same girl was at its height. In fact they were, at the moment Tony arrived, engaged in a street brawl and Olin had drawn a knife to attack Bennie. Tony intervened. The two fighters fled and Tony was left alone when the police arrived. They promptly arrested him and took him to jail. He was allowed to contact Victor, who hired an attorney and soon had him freed.

Victor owned three Rolls Royce cars: a tan one, a black one, and a white one. He kept them in the three cities which he frequented most: New York, Chicago, and Detroit. Tony, the chauffeur, dressed accordingly, a tan uniform when he drove the tan car, a black uniform and a white uniform for the other two. One day, when Tony was driving the tan Rolls Royce, Olin spotted him and remembered him as the one who had intervened in his fight. He called the police and trailed the tan car until the police came.

"This here guy," he told the arresting officer, "is the guilty one. You arrested him and then set him loose. He pulled a knife on me and he is guilty as hell. You'se had better keep him this time. And who's that guy he drives for? 'Count' Victor

Lustig, that's who he is. (Unfortunately, Tony had boasted to Bennie about his connection.) You'se had better keep him this time or I'll bust you too." The police hauled Tony off to jail, told him to tell them where 'Count' Victor Lustig was or they'd lock him up. Tony refused and was accordingly put in the slammer for the second time.

Again, Victor hired an attorney. He had to keep out of the fray this time since the police now had his name. This time it cost him $10,000 to make enough pay-offs to free his chauffeur.

Lustig decided that Olin would make a good mark, that he needed a good dressing down for all he had cost him. His brother Emil was with him in Chicago. Emil, although not always dependable, was a good actor and a good sleuth. Since neither he nor Tony could safely appear in this scheme, he sent Emil to investigate Olin Starkey. Lustig thoroughly investigated every mark before he approached him. He would find out about his religion, politics, financial and marital status, his age and names of his children and grandchildren. He had to be scrutinized for some time right down to his favorite wine and shaving lotion. Several failures in his early days taught him this procedure.

Emil found out that the produce king's cigar stands, the backs of saloons and barber shops, were fronts for 'illegals' such as bookies, bootleg liquor and gambling. They decided that Olin was ripe for deception and was ready for the money box. Victor wouldn't attempt to get him on the bookies, for he feared he knew more about horse racing than he did, but the money box would be the thing. A man of illegal stature would always be ready to make more money.

"I'll get him for $50,000," Victor decided. "The old fellow has plenty with all his illegal transactions. And you, Emil, will do the leg work."

Emil was always game. So they dressed him up in old clothes, put him in a huckster's wagon and sent him to Olin to buy potatoes.

"That's more than I can pay," Emil told the king when the latter gave him the price of his potatoes. "I'm a poor man and only want to make enough money to set up a stand and sell potatoes. I want to make enough money so that I can make more money."

"What ye mean by that?" Olin asked, "Make enough money to make more money?"

"Well, you see, I know a man who has a box that makes money. I want to buy it and make money. Ya see?"

"No, I don't see. I never seen a box that makes money and ya never did either. The only way to make money is to get out and work for it the way I do. Yer pullin' my leg just to get a cheaper price on my potatoes. Yer might as well give up right now. There's no such thing as a box that makes money."

"I'll bet you $10,000 and I can prove it to you."

"I'll take yer bet, but where are you going to get the money to pay me when I win the bet? Ye ain't got enough money to buy potatoes."

"I'll get it, but I'm not going to lose! The fellow that has the money making machine is a 'Count', a big fellow."

"A 'Count', ye say. I've heard about that 'Count' that's around here before. Take me to him. I'd like to see a real 'Count.'" He had visions of turning this 'Count' over to the police and reaping a big haul.

"Indeed not. He wouldn't even see you. He's too big for you."

"How'd you get in with him? Ye can't do anything I can't do. Ye ain't got any money. Ye ain't got enough to buy potatoes. How'd ye get in touch with him?"

"Oh, I have my ways," Emil answered. "He's a countryman of mine. He'd see me when he wouldn't see you."

"Aw, come on. Take me to him." He pulled his wallet from his pocket and extracted a $5 bill. "I'll give you this if you take me to this 'Count' and yer bet is still good." He pushed the bill into Emil's hand.

Emil softened. "Well, I'll try. But no promises. This count never sees any one except me, his countryman, and a few other fellows."

Emil got into his huckster's wagon and turned to leave.

"Here, ye ain't got yer potatoes. I'll give the damn things to ye cause yer goin' to take me to this 'Count.'"

Emil returned to Victor with a load of potatoes. Victor was in his hotel room with Roberta and their daughter.

"There's a load of potatoes down on the street. What'll I do with them? And the mark wants to see you."

"Take the potatoes and give them to the hotel chef and tell the mark that I don't have time to see him. And remember, you are 'Karl', not Emil anymore." Emil was disappointed. All this work and now no interest on the part of his brother. Besides, he had $10,000 at stake (if he could collect such a bet).

"Aren't you going to see the poor slob?"

"Well, tell him I haven't much time for him. I'm on my way to Europe and I'll be checking out of this hotel tomorrow. Bring him around by five o'clock."

Emil, now Karl, went to see the mark in a battered old car this time.

"He'll see you for a short time this evening. But I warn you. He probably won't show you the money box and that's why you want to see him. He's a queer guy. A 'Count' can afford to be, you know. He doesn't talk much and he'll say little to you. Besides, you can't see him dressed like you are now. You'll have to improve your talk. No gutter talk to this 'Count', you know. If you spoil this for me, I'll get you some day. No loud mouthing!"

Olin was ready to say or do anything, so eager was he to see the 'Count' and the money box and to turn 'Count Lustig' into the police. The two approached the hotel at 10 minutes to five that evening. As they went in, ten minutes early, Tony and a new chauffeur who had been hired for the occasion, since Tony dared not appear before Olin, were just leaving the hotel. Emil's carelessness in keeping an appointment at the designated time almost cost them the deal. Olin thought he recognized the chauffeur who had punched him, although Tony was wearing a black uniform as he was driving the black Rolls Royce and his back was turned.

"Who were those guys?" Olin asked. 'Karl' hastened him to the hotel room and avoided answering the question. "Now don't spoil things by saying the wrong thing. You'd better let me do the talking."

'Karl' knocked on the door of Victor's hotel room. Victor answered and coldly showed them into the room.

"Gentlemen, what can I do for you? I haven't much time as I am checking out of this hotel and won't be in Chicago very long. I am sailing for Europe."

Olin forgot himself for a moment. "Who were those guys we saw leaving just now," he demanded surlily.

Victor stiffened and turned to 'Karl'. "Take your friend out of here. I don't talk to people like him."

"I'm so sorry, 'Count'. Give him a chance. He won't talk like that again, I promise."

Olin kept pleading, "Oh, I'm just a dumb American. Forgive me, Count. I'm sorry."

"Well, one more chance. You have already spoiled my evening's plans. I'm doing this as special favor to you, Karl" he said turning to 'Karl' and motioning them to chairs.

Emil started talking. "Is it all right for you to tell us about the magic box?"

"Yes, but it's gone up. It's $50,000 now. I'm leaving for Europe and don't have time to waste on you and your friend."

Emil appeared dumbfounded. "I couldn't possibly get that much money together."

"That's your problem. I'm sorry."

"May my friend talk to you about it? Will you describe it to him?" Emil continued, "It's a box so constructed that you can put in one bill and blank pieces of paper and as many bills will come out as you have put in blank pieces of paper. You know, Count, I just must buy that machine. Won't you let me see it work again?" Emil pleaded.

"Where'll you get the money? You won't get $50,000 selling potatoes, Karl, my boy."

"But, I thought it was only $25,000 and here today you say it is $50,000?!"

"Please sir, can't we see it?" Olin put in.

"No." Victor was playing the waiting game as he did with all his marks. "No, I'm hungry and can't take time to show you anything. I'm going to eat."

"Can we join you?" Emil responded.

"Yes, you can be my guests."

He went to the phone and asked to have his car sent around. It was there in a few minutes with the new chauffeur driving it. They went to a nearby restaurant and ordered their meal. Victor was silent and reserved. Emil tried to keep up the conversation, but with little success.

Their meal finished, Victor paid the bill, called Tony and told him to send the car around with the new driver. The three men went out to the waiting car.

"Where would you gentlemen like to be dropped off?" Victor asked as they entered the car.

"Oh, Count, we would like to see, you know what. (The new driver must, of course, not hear anything about the money box). Won't you show it to us now that you have eaten and are no longer hungry?" Emil pleaded.

"Well, all right. Come up to my hotel room."

It had been arranged that Tony, who had the box, and who was waiting for a call, would come to the hotel and bring the box. There was a knock on the door. Victor answered and brought in a package. Moving slowly, he placed it on the dressing table. Out of a leather case, he took a rich rosewood box, polished and shining with its brass trim. It was already set up with the money in it.

He told his eager listeners that the 12 hours required to make the counterfeit bills was about up, that he had put a $100 bill in it early that morning along with nine pieces of blank paper the size of a bill. He talked slowly and went about the whole affair methodically. He took his large gold watch out of his vest pocket, slowly opened the lid and looked at the time. He stroked the box as he held the open watch in his hand.

"One has to be very careful about the time. In a moment now, the 12 hours will have expired."

He snapped the watch shut, put it back in his pocket and turned the crank of the box. Out came the bills as he had predicted, 10 one hundred dollar bills. He slowly put the $1000 in bills in his wallet and proceded to put the box back in its case.

"There it is gentlemen. A precious box, I assure you, one for which I would not part with for less than $50,000. Since you don't have that much money, Karl, that must end our negotiations today. I must go and prepare for my trip to Europe."

"But I still want to buy it," Emil expostulated.

"Where will you get the money, my friend?" Lustig asked, looking at him coldly with his steel gray eyes.

"I've got some and my friend here, Olin Starkey, will lend me some, won't you, sir."

"I can give you the whole $50,000 and I want to buy it," Olin said hastily, his words jumping over each other in his haste and greed to get his hands on this magic money-making box.

"But I want to buy it, too!" Emil kept up the subterfuge.

"Gentlemen, this is a 12 hour box. It takes 12 hours to make new money. Come back in 12 hours with the money and the box is yours. I won't be here, but I'll let Karl know where I'll be."

Emil and Olin left, the latter insisting that he had $50,000 and wanted the magic box. Emil still simulated a quarrel. "No, I want it. You pay half and I'll pay half and it will belong to both of us."

"No go. Where'd we keep it?" Olin asked.

"In a bank deposit box."

"And neither of us could get it out without the other one being there."

"No go, to that. God damn you, I've got the money and you've got nothing but potatoes you get from me. Give me the box. I'll pay for it and I'll keep it."

"No you won't. I want it. I won't take you to the Count."

"I'll go myself."

"You can't. He doesn't live in that hotel and you don't know where he is. In 12 hours the money must come out, so we'll skip it all since we can't agree."

Olin was desperate. "No, we can't."

Emil thought for a moment. "Remember, you have a bet on with me. I bet you $10,000 that the box would work. You pay me $10,000 and I'll let you buy the money box."

Emil came back to the produce huckster the next morning, just hours before the 12 hours were up. Olin was nervous.

"Calm down now." he said. "You got the money? Give me my $10,000 and I'll take you to the money box."

"Take me to my bank and I'll get the money, $10,000 for you and $50,000 for the box."

By the time they had the money, the 12 hours were about up. They rushed into 'Count' Lustig's new hotel room just in time. Victor eyed them coldly.

"I thought you weren't coming. I'm leaving in a few minutes and could not have waited any longer."

The room was empty of all personal effects, a sign that he was leaving immediately. The box was on a table in front of him, set up with the first 10 bills.

"I've got the $50,000 and want to buy the money box. Here, give it to me."

Olin was used to money doing the talking and was disappointed that Victor didn't seem to be in a hurry to get the money in his hands.

"Shall I demonstrate?" He turned the crank and ground out 10, $100 bills, one of which was the original.

A doubt flashed through Olin's head. "Are you sure these could be cashed at a bank? I'll bet you'd be arrested if you tried."

Again he had to cringe under the steel-gray gaze of 'Count' Victor Lustig. "You doubt me? I should throw you out. We'll go to a bank at once and cash these bills!" The three men walked to the bank which was nearby.

"Karl, you cash the bills."

Emil went to a cage and handed the cashier a $100 bill and got five $20 bills in return. Pre-instructed by his brother, he went to another cage to cash another bill, and so on until six of the bills were cashed.

He stopped Emil then and turned to Olin. "Never cash more than one counterfeit bill at the same window. Now, we shall go to another bank to make sure the bills can be cashed."

"No, no, I am convinced," Olin protested. "We'll cash them all here." Emil continued until all nine bills had been cashed.

They must hurry now, for Victor's time to leave for Europe was almost here. They went back to the hotel, where Tony, guarding the box, had in the meantime placed it on the table. Olin paid Lustig the $50,000 and left with the magic box. Victor sent Tony to bring the car around. He and Emil got in the car and the three set out for Kansas to visit Roberta's family.

Victor Lustig never followed up on his marks. What they did when they found out they were duped, he never knew. How Olin Starkey took his loss of $50,000 plus the $10,000 bet was never known. But a mark they found in St. Louis shortly after did try to investigate.

A group of friends, Dapper Dan Collins, Fritz Lang, Nickie Arnstein, Emil and Victor were enjoying an afternoon in Tom Kearney's tobacco shop in St. Louis. Tom was not there. They met a man named Kallie in the shop and in the exchange of pleasantries and drinks, Dapper Dan told Kallie about the magic money box.

"There are three kinds of them. Vic has them all. $15,000 will buy you one that is good for a year, $20,000 for a two-year one, and $50,000 for one that will last a lifetime. I suspect those life-time ones. How can you know it will last a lifetime if you don't live that long?"

Kallie was interested. All the men joined in singing the praises of the money box which could put money in your pocket and in your debtor's pocket, although it would be counterfeit money. It was so good that it could never be detected. Kallie thought that it wouldn't have time to be detected in his pockets. He owed so much it would go faster than any detection. The men who had started to talk as a joke, looked knowingly at each other. Here was a good mark. He was so deep in debt that he would do anything to get out of it.

It all ended in Kallie's leaving $15,000, which only increased his indebtedness that much, and taking the money box with him to his home in Detroit. It was loaded with real bills, six of them with the last number changed on each of them, and the first trial of the magic box was successful. The second try proved fruitless. Kallie, being a man of ingenuity with his hands, took the box apart to find out what was wrong and remedy it. When he found that he couldn't make anything out of it, he called Tom Kearney in St. Louis and asked him how he could get in touch with the man who sold him the machine. Tom was angry.

"I've told you many times, Vic, that I don't approve of your business and I don't ever want you to pull off anything in my shop. Let this be the last time."

Victor called Kallie by telephone.

"What is the matter, sir? You were trying to contact me. Didn't the box work?"

"Oh, yes, sir, it worked fine the first time and I got the money out of it. But now it won't work. I must have done something wrong. I took the box apart to see if I could fix it. Now I can't put it back together again. Can you tell me what to do? Maybe I can make one just like it since this one was to last only a year."

"I am afraid you have ruined the box," Victor said in a mournful tone.

"What? You mean it can't be fixed and I'll never be able to pay my bills? Can't you tell me something to do?"

"No, it's impossible to repair those boxes. Their delicate mechanism when once disturbed, can never be put in place again. The only thing to do is buy a new one."

Oh! was almost a scream over the phone and moved Victor. "I'll tell you what I will do. The box cost me $10,000. I made a profit of $5,000 on it. I'll give you my profit. Will that help you? Tell me where to send it."

"I guess it will have to," and Victor heard the receiver drop as the victim on the other end whispered out an address.

NINE

O N ONE OF their earlier trips to Europe, Roberta met a woman who later became a good friend. She had wanted to become a friend of Senator George's wife earlier, but circumstances forbade that. This time she insisted that nothing should interfere to curtail their friendship, which began with a desire to help the woman.

On the first night out on the Andania, she saw a woman who, she decided, was an older version of herself on her first trip on ship, not knowing what or how to do the proper things, to observe the proper protocol. The woman, Emma, was alone. Roberta had Victor to tell her what to do, but Emma, alone, had no one to tell her. Roberta struck up a friendship with her for this very reason. Emma was dressed lavishly, but in poor taste. She broke a string of genuine pearls she was wearing and laughingly said, when asked if she had them all, "What's a pearl or two?" and "I wonder why those knots are there." Adults can be as cruel as children at times and a few of them laughed at the woman's apparent ignorance of pearls.

Emma was an oil-rich widow from Oklahoma. She and her husband had been poor dirt farmers when oil was discovered on their land and the childless couple found themselves suddenly rich. Emma's husband was an intelligent man and made a will to take care of their wealth in case of death. All of the land should go to Emma, unencumbered as long as she lived. And at her death it was to go to his family, brothers and sisters, who lived on adjoining oil lands and had already gained wealth. Since Emma, Arkansas born, had no family or near relatives, the will was a fair and just division of property after Emma's death. But, she confided to Roberta soon after they had met, three of her brothers-in-law had, the next day after her husband's death, induced her to sign over to them three of the biggest wells on the lease. When she looked back now, she couldn't understand why she did it. She was just grieving so much for her dear husband, the only friend she had ever had in her life, that she didn't realize what she was doing, especially since the brothers-in-law had convinced her at the time that she wouldn't be able to manage the wells and might lose them.

Victor and Roberta were traveling as 'Count' and 'Countess Von Kessler', so had prestige on the ship. They ate at the Captain's table and had one of the best cabins. As Roberta's desire to help Emma grew, friendship grew too. She invited Emma to the Captain's table with them. There, she had done a little bragging about the number of oil wells she owned in Oklahoma. 'Count' Von Kessler eyed her sharply and listened attentively. That night he said to his wife: "That old lady has money. I'm going to clip her."

"Over my dead body!" Roberta said. "She's a good woman, an honest woman and you leave her alone." Victor Lustig's wife had grown in courage since the day when she politely refused the invitation of the wife of Senator George to luncheon, for fear it would displease her husband.

Victor knew that he dared not go ahead with his scheme and, by the time the boat docked, he had learned to like the woman too.

Roberta kept in contact with her in Paris, took her to see the Eiffel Tower, one of Roberta's favorite spots, where she could look down and see the smallness of the world. Before they parted, she invited Emma to visit her in New York, when they would have their apartment open again. She would contact her and tell her when to come, for she never left an address with anyone.

Emma eventually came to New York. Roberta took her shopping, helped her choose the right clothing for a lady of her means and stature, and took her to the opera. Emma was still lamenting the oil wells which her brothers-in-law had virtually stolen from her. She wondered if there was anything she could do to get her land back. Victor saw three good marks in the Oklahoma oil well transactions and promised to help her. It would take time though, and he wouldn't even venture an approximate time. He knew nothing about oil wells or the stock market, so closely connected with the discovery of oil in Oklahoma. He studied it, learned all the terminology of oil development and spent time in the stock market to find out how it worked. He left no word that belonged to the oil business unstudied, just as he studied every mark before he took action. It was six months before he notified Emma that he and Roberta would visit her in Oklahoma. After their arrival, he unfolded his plans. He would get her land with the oil wells back for Emma and something for himself in compensation for the work and time he had put into the scheme.

Emma was to have a big dinner and invite all her relatives, including the three brothers-in-law, to meet 'Count' and 'Countess Von Kessler'. Their amazement at seeing a real count and countess in Oklahoma and, in all places, at Emma's home, carried them away and they forgot, for a moment, their own self interests. The 'Count' explained his presence in their state.

Oklahoma was becoming known in the East, even throughout the world as the great oil-producing state. He had decided that the future money market was in Oklahoma and he wanted to get in on it. He came to invest in oil lands.

Emma spoke up, "I'm going to sell him all my land. I'm tired of this drab life with nothing but oil day and night to look at, to talk about, living out here on this lonesome lease."

She wanted to see things in New York and Paris. She had gone to the top of the Eiffel Tower and thought it the most wonderful experience she had ever had. If she sold all of her land with the big oil wells on it, the biggest oil wells in Oklahoma, she was sure she would have plenty money to see the world. Why stay here and put her money in the bank when she could be enjoying it so much. Her good friend, 'Count Von Kessler', wanted to buy it all and there was nothing to keep her from selling.

The house erupted! The in-laws saw all of their fortune disappearing. If she sold, she would spend all of the money and there would be nothing left to them at her death. Their future depended on her keeping the land.

"You can't do this, you can't do this," they cried as they pushed each other around trying to get to Emma. Victor waved a paper at them, trying to stop the confusion. "This is my agreement with Emma. She has signed it and she has to keep her word. I came here to buy this land and you're not going to stop me. Emma can do what she pleases with her land as long as she lives."

Confusion went on until in the morning hours. Finally, the three brothers-in-law got in a huddle and came up with the request that they wait until the next day and perhaps something could be worked out.

"Early tomorrow morning," Victor insisted. "I can't wait one moment longer and I want my land. I have the money and the signed agreement. You can't stop me."

Emma was ready to capitulate. "I want my land back that you took from me, that's all I want. I don't care whether I sell or not," she said to the three brothers-in-law.

"But I want my land that you agreed to sell to me," Victor yelled back at Emma. "I'll sue you if you don't keep this agreement. Let's sleep on it now and start again tomorrow morning."

"You and your wife stay here with me the rest of the night." Emma was nervous. Things had gone further than she had anticipated and she wasn't sure about the 'Von Kesslers'. She told her brothers-in-law she was afraid they might go to town and come back with the sheriff.

"We'll stay too," the three gentlemen said. So Emma bedded them all as best she could.

When they met the next morning, cooler and more in possession of themselves, the brothers-in-law, encouraged by Emma's saying all she wanted was her land back, made this offer to Emma:

"If you will sign an agreement not to sell for 90 days, we will give you your land back."

"No, no," from Victor. "She signed this agreement and she has to keep it. I'll sue."

"If they give me my land back, how much would you ask to settle with them?" Emma turned to Victor with this new idea which had apparently come to her.

"No, all or nothing. I want my land."

The men grasped at the little straw Emma was throwing to them. "We'll give you $25,000 and give her her land back if you will tear up that agreement."

"No, not enough, not enough."

Emma feigned a pleading tome. "Would you settle for $50,000 and my land back?"

The count appeared to do some calculating. "Well, since you are my good friend and you want your land back so badly, I'll consider $50,000. But you'll have to get it right away this morning or I'll insist on keeping the agreement."

"We'll take it."

They went out and in a short time came back with $50,000. Emma presented them with a pre-arranged and pre-written agreement that they would return the land to her that they had taken from her. The 'Count' and 'Countess' went back to New York, satisfied with their dip in the Oklahoma oil fields. Emma stayed on her lease, but she remained a good friend with the 'Von Kesslers' for many years, even travelling to Europe with them at times.

Another Oklahoma oil baron eventually came into Lustig's life. Roberta's diary doesn't say when or where Victor first met Ty (Titanic) Thompson, whose real name was Alvin Clarence Thomas. Ty Thompson was a gambler; a big gambler. He bet on anything, large or small. Once he was sitting in the lobby of a hotel with another gambler friend. To pass the time, he said, "I'll bet more women than men will enter this hotel in the next two hours." The bet was on and Ty was losing, when suddenly 200 women came in. He never would acknowledge whether he knew about the ladies' convention that was scheduled to meet there or not.

Once when another gambler was bragging about his golf prowess and his big wins, Titanic said he could drive a golf ball 400 yards. The bet was taken and Titanic took a ball and went out to a lake that was frozen over. It was in the dead of winter in Connecticut. He teed off and the last time he talked about it, he thought the ball might still be rolling!

In his golf gambling, he would pretend he couldn't play or played badly, so that the gamblers would bet on the other fellow and he would win. In the beginning, the bigger the bet, the poorer he played until he knew for certain that the results would be worthwhile for him. Then the game would change and the winnings were his.

Ty Thompson got his soubriquet from a gambling partner in a crap game, when he won $800. The loser, who had not caught his name said, "Stay away from that Thompson. He'll sink you like the Titanic." He was Titanic Thompson from then on.

He taught Victor how to play golf; that is, he did the finishing job. Vic had become a good golf player without ever having a lesson from a professional. When he decided he wanted to learn the game, he hired a caddy and asked him to point out the best of the golfers playing that course. For a month, he followed the caddy as he trailed the good players. He bought the best set of clubs on the market. He claimed the caddy was his teacher and his grip was perfected by the caddy. Finally, he began trailing Ty Thompson and eventually joined him. Ty finished his golf lessons and made an excellent golfer out of him.

Titanic admired Victor for having learned golf without a pro and Lustig probably admired Ty for his heroism at the sinking of 'the' ship. He was making the ship crossing as usual, gambling and known only as Alvin Clarence Thomas. He had just experienced a big win when the ship suddenly stood still around the midnight hour.

"What the hell?!?"

"Nothing's wrong, you can't stop now!" his gambling partner answered fearfully, seeing his chances for the night vanishing if the game stopped.

"Hell, yes I can! Ships don't just stop in the middle of the night out in the water if there's not something wrong."

After this introduction, Titanic would launch into the story of that fatal night. After lowering all the women into life boats and hearing the cries of the steerage that were left behind, Ty began grabbing one person after another and throwing them into the collapsables that were being lowered into the water. Then, when the last collapsable had been lowered and the great Titanic was going down, Ty, with a whole wall of men, jumped overboard into the icy waters. He caught a raft and was picked up by another boat that came to their rescue.

Victor and Titanic, both gamblers, had one common trait: Titanic never bet with an amateur or one who, he knew, couldn't win, and Victor never swindled an honest man or a poor man.

After many years when he and Victor exchanged bets or were partners at all the race tracks, losing and winning, Titanic turned to oil when Lustig was turning more and more to capers. Ty's oil gamble struck pay dirt, and Alvin Thomas became an oil baron in Oklahoma, playing golf instead of horses or cards.

But just as Victor could never give up his swindling successes, Alvin Thomas could never give up completely his gambling yens and entertained his friends with little spur-of-the moment bets, which he always won.

TEN

ROBERTA LUSTIG IN her diary described the man simply as 'the Banker', a horrible man who had come up from poverty by every illegal means possible. Now, he was president of the bank in a small Kansas town. He had actually sent innocent friends to prison for crimes they had never committed, altered records, and misplaced files. He foreclosed on poor farmers minutes before they scraped together the money to pay off a mortgage. Now, Victor had been told, he was in serious trouble. He had used too many of the bank's funds, the only bank in the small town, and could not pay them back. He faced foreclosure just as so many farmers had faced it because of his greed.

Victor found him to be an easy mark, ready to listen to any scheme that would make money for himself. Victor had researched his background before ever approaching him and he had but one desire: to expose this fraud and make him suffer for all the misdeeds of his life. Victor told his wife and she put it in her diary. He spoke of the man with absolute disgust, the diary says. He noted the man's clenched hands and half shut eyes as he anticipated this illegal scheme that 'Count' Lustig unfolded to him. It made no difference to him that it was illegal if it would mean money, millions, as the 'Count' told him, if he would pursue the plan.

He was quite impressed with the 'Count' and invited him to dinner. Lustig followed his usual scheme of being slow about divulging the whole plan after he had enticed the mark to a certain point of greed that could break his back.

There was a large vacant building in a town a short distance away and the whole scheme revolved around this area. 'The Banker' was to borrow $150,000 from 'his' bank and other sources which, he assured Lustig, would never be missed. With these funds, a new bank was to be opened. Lustig was to bring in the staff in a scheme which, he told 'the Banker', had been worked before and always proved successful. In fact, it was failure proof. The staff would substitute counterfeit money and the $150,000 was simply a cover-up in case the law found out anything. He would recover his $150,000 and much more in five days or less and he would never be seen. He would have no connection with the new bank. It would be Lustig who would suffer if the law got it.

The scheme would last no more than five days. All the money that would be deposited by the public, and it would be no small amount, for there was no other bank in that town, would be divided between Lustig and 'the Banker'. Then Lustig would disappear, the bank close, and 'the Banker' would have made his millions. They discussed the remodeling of the building and instant furnishings right down to the last ink well. 'The Banker' surprised Lustig by walking out of the room and returning with $15,000 in one hundred dollar bills. Lustig said he would begin the refurbishing at once and left 'the Banker's' home.

A large van pulled up to the building Lustig had leased beforehand and twelve men got to work, cleaning and painting, installed carpeting, furnishings, supplies and two beautifully executed signs: 'Open an account of $500 on opening day and get a free set of bone china dinner service for four.'

When the furnishings were completed, the 'Count' called 'the Banker', purposely about dusk, and invited him over to see the new bank whose opening was to be Monday morning. This was a Friday night, so the signs had to be placed in the window immediately that people might see them on Saturday when they went to town or on their way to and from church Sunday morning.

'The Banker' was so delighted with things that he suggested they go by the bank and get the money for the opening day. Lustig insisted that there was no rush, he was tired, needed to go to bed and could wait until the next day, Saturday. But 'the Banker' insisted "now". Lustig finally let himself be convinced. They walked into the darkened lobby, and the banker proceeded to open the vault, count out the money, put it in a green bag and hand it to Lustig.

"Now my friend, you can go get your rest." 'The Banker' drove 'Count' Lustig to his hotel. He went in calmly, rode the elevator to his room, stuffed his belongings into two laundry bags, took them and the green bag containing the $150,000 to a pre-cased window, dropped them down into the alley, went down to the hotel desk and asked the boy at the desk if there were an all-night restaurant. He departed with a bow and a smile to everyone in the lobby. Outside, he went immediately to the alley, picked up his laundry bags and the green bag, got into a car, pre-arranged to meet him in the alley, and was driven away. Fifty miles away he got into his own limousine, with Tony at the wheel and went home to his family to prepare for another trip to Europe.

A pre-arranged crew came into the bank building and removed all the furnishings. 'The Banker' was left to stew in his own misdeeds with Lustig out of sight.

The whole operation had taken less than five days. The research and the plans with the various crews had taken several months. But he used the furnishings many times over in similar schemes and at the most they did not cost more than $25,000. He finally sold them at only a ten percent depreciation.

The trip to Europe was one of many. He always took the family with him in those early days, but they never 'traveled' as a family. Roberta would travel as a young widow with a child. And he? Well, they never knew just who or how he would be.

Roberta and Betty Jean seldom saw him when they were on ship, but he was always standing where he could see them. Sometimes he would pass them by and tip his hat. He never outwardly knew them but he would come to their stateroom at night and return to his own by dawn.

"This time we are going to Europe so that my father can enjoy his granddaughter," Victor told his wife. The child of Victor and Roberta Lustig grew up in luxury. Roberta was considered the Cinderella of the family by her relatives and they used her in every way they could. Betty, in her turn, used her parents as much as she could. She loved them very much and didn't know what she would do without them, but she demanded everything she wanted and was refused nothing. In after life, when she had to work to support her children, she spoke of her childhood thus:

"It seemed as though God always dangled the goodies of life before me and just as I could reach up to take them, would snatch them away. I even felt that God was laughing at me for all I had and all I had missed in life."

Her schooling was intermittent, of course, considering the kind of life they led, running from one place to the next and frustrating all of Roberta's plans to have a home. She always had a tutor, but the tutor had to be changed so many times that one could hardly begin where the other left off.

Now on the way to grandfather's, there was little chance for the tutor to act. They arrived in Cherbourg in January, 1926. Grandfather Lustig met them at the railroad station and immediately took his little grandchild in his arms. Betty remembers the soft touch of his coat and the tender way he picked her up; tenderness from a big, forceful man.

He immediately loved his only grandchild. She loved him just as quickly and told him she wanted to stay with him forever. Grandfather's hair was closely cropped, nearly all white, and he had retained a little of his tan from the summer which he had spent in the South of France. He had learned a little more English and told his granddaughter in her language that he loved her. He swept her up and swung her around and around, then tenderly cuddled her in his arms as she snuggled against his fur collar.

He put her down, embraced her mother and grabbed his son's hand. After looking at each other for a moment, they too embraced. Victor and his father were never sure of each other. The father wanted so desperately to hold on to this son and hoped, each time he saw him, that he had reformed his life.

Grandfather looked around him now and said, "Where are they?" He meant Grace and Tony, who had accompanied them on an earlier visit. "Not this time,"

Victor answered his father. Misunderstanding the answer, the old man again embraced his son. "Then this time you will stay. You will never leave me again." Victor tried to explain that Tony and Grace were enjoying a vacation of their own and was probably saved from a more embarrassing explanation by Betty, who kept tugging at his sleeve to be picked up. The older Lustig picked her up, turned his back on his son and his wife and walked away toward the waiting car. He silently opened the back door of the car and silently motioned Roberta to get in, putting Betty in the front seat. Victor came running with the luggage boy. They bestowed the luggage in a waiting truck, which Grandfather had brought, remembering the amount of luggage of past times. The older man got behind the wheel of the waiting car, pulled Betty toward him and gave her a kiss. Victor jumped in the car next to his wife and the man at the wheel ignored him, as he drove off, looking straight ahead, his lips tight, and his hands clutching the wheel, in what might have been a mental stranglehold of his son's throat. Off they went in silence for some time. Finally, Ludwig Lustig spoke in German to his son. They would visit friends on their way to Zurich.

In every house in which they stopped, they found the happiness of family life. There were children to play with and beautiful gardens to play in.

Victor announced that he must go to Paris on business and told Roberta she could go along. "Absolutely not," she said. "I will stay here." Grandfather was upset but he did not speak up in anger this time.

"Please, Vic, no, please."

Victor said nothing but kept on packing and left early the next morning.

Grandfather, his daughter-in-law and his grandchild continued on their journey, stopping at more homes to pay brief visits, but it wasn't the same without Victor. After another day and a half the three of them left for Paris. Roberta wanted to shop, and Betty wanted to go up in the Eiffel Tower. Grandfather took her up and she looked down at all those tiny people down there.

They visited more friends of grandfather and Betty met many little children who took her to their toy rooms and let her play with their toys. Betty always remembered the visit in Zurich. She remembered sleeping in a huge feather bed which seemed to billow around her and make her feel like she was swimming on feathers. She could look out through a colored glass window, put her hand out one of the small openings and see her fingers dance in a maze of colors.

This was her window. Grandfather had it made especially for her, he told her, and it would be 'hers' forever in 'her' room, in Zurich. He was still hoping that his son would settle down and continue his business. Betty remembered the beautiful blue birds and the flowers in the window. She remembered three names mingled in the green leaves: Jeanne, Betty, Dominique. Those were the names he had registered in the family bible in Zurich. He felt sorry for Roberta, who said she had but one name.

It was beautiful living with grandfather and she wanted to stay forever. She could remember a trip across a bridge to Prague, Czechoslovakia, and hearing her grandfather say: "Your father was born here."

"On the bridge?" his granddaughter exclaimed!

"No, in Prague," the old man said tenderly. He wanted to love his son and be proud of him. Victor loved him too and always regretted bringing disgrace upon him. But his love of adventure was greater than his love for his father.

Ludwig Lustig's heart was breaking. No son to pass on the proud name of Lustig. Emil, the younger son, was a failure and his Viktor, a scandal to the name.

Betty also remembered a voice on this trip to Europe. That voice was the voice of her grandfather saying in German: "We shall rule the world some day." Her mother recoiled and held her child closer. She dreaded another war and wanted to get away from this atmosphere of superiority. She contacted her husband and they left abruptly; leaving a four-year old, spoiled American girl regretting that she could not stay forever in this grandfather land. The next time she would see her grandfather, he would carry her out of a Paris hotel room and put her on a ship for America.

Divorce and a war ended the happy reunions of a little girl and her stately grandfather who may have seen, in this child, the possible future he had lost in his two sons.

ELEVEN

THEY RETURNED TO America and went to Kansas with Victor looking forward to a visit with Paul, his brother-in-law. They were great friends, although a world apart in professions. Paul was a trainman, an engineer. On this visit, after their return from visiting Grandfather Lustig in Europe, Victor rode the train with Paul, got grease on his immaculate clothes and enjoyed himself in every way.

It was their last night in Kansas. Roberta was still the Cinderella of this Kansas town and Victor was their hero. Relatives and neighbors had assembled in Paul's and half-sister Ethel's home for their farewell night. Victor entertained them with tales of American and European history. He was not an American citizen, but he knew American history better than most natives. History was another of his passions along with swindling and trains. He had a clipping with him that a friend had sent him from Paris. It was regarding the Eiffel tower. It was getting quite rusted, the clipping said, and city officials wondered if it was worth the cost of repairing it, if it meant that much to the people of Paris. Built to be only temporary during the world exposition, should they retain it now?

"I doubt if the people of Paris are that fond of the Tower," Lustig had added after reading the clipping.

There was a gasp among his listeners. Roberta was the loudest. "Don't let them tear it down, Victor. I love that Tower. You know how I do."

Lustig was quick to seize the opportunity, like a journalist, to use this bit of news as a peg on which to keep the attention of his audience.

"Do we have anything in America that we would like to see torn down? Is there anything in this town that nobody likes and would just as soon see destroyed?"

Different old houses were suggested, but there was always someone who saw some historical or economic value to it. The evening closed on a pleasant note and the Lustigs left the next day to go to St. Louis to visit the Kearneys. There was business as usual, but Roberta was not enthusiastic about it.

She had never wanted for anything. Victor kept sums of money in lock boxes in every major city of the United States and Roberta kept the keys. But money did not suffice, she was beginning to realize. She wondered what a normal life would be like and decided she couldn't keep this up much longer. She was tired of her insecure, restless life. Victor left her in the hotel in St. Louis while he went to see Tom, promising to be back to take her to dinner. Tom invited Victor and another friend, Mike O'Neil, to dinner and Victor went, forgetting all about Roberta. This had happened before of late, all of which added to her dissatisfaction.

During the dinner, Lustig became interested in what O'Neil told him. He had been a building contractor, but had changed his profession. He was in the salvage business and was amazed at the profit it was bringing him.

Lustig's interest brought out a description of the work, how they went into the building to be demolished and took out everything that was removable: plumbing fixtures, hardware, doors, light fixtures, hardwood floors, etc. These were all valuable on the market and brought an extra profit to the salvage dealer. Then the demolition would begin and the materials salvageable sold or used again. It was a great business, Mike O'Neil said.

The evening wore on and Bertie, sitting in the hotel room, was entirely forgotten. Grace had put Betty to bed and Roberta was fully dressed for dinner. She waited until after eight o'clock and then began to build up her anger. She drank the wine they had in the hotel room and by the time Victor got back, she was half intoxicated and as angry as she could possibly be. He remained silent in her storm and did not tell her that he had been with friends, while she was angrily accusing him of being out with another woman. She might have forgiven him, had he spoken up, but he didn't and her jealousy raged. It was a case of two stubborn people tearing themselves to shreds.

Roberta took Grace and Betty and left for Kansas City. She filed for divorce and in her pique, she married a Charles Gibson. She regretted it as soon as the ring was placed upon her finger.

After the divorce proceedings had gone through, Victor came to Kansas City to claim his visiting rights and see his daughter. He was registered at the Hotel Crillon in Paris for April 3 to April 21, but something more important occupied his mind right now. One day, he claimed to take Betty out for ice cream and the merry-go-round. Instead, he took her to Europe, hired a maid and installed them in the Hotel Crillon. In New York, he had stopped to purchase an entirely new wardrobe for Betty and booked passage to Europe. Tony went with Lustig and his daughter as usual. Also waiting their arrival in Paris were Robert Arthur Tourbillion, known as Dapper Dan, and Victor's brother, Emil. Victor Lustig took Dapper Dan along because of his fluency in French, which he had learned long ago from his French parents. Also awaiting his arrival was a Frenchman, Maurice Rosseau; a man who was to die of cancer the following year. He had a wife and two children and was frantic about their futures when he learned of his impending death.

The four men, Lustig, Emil, Dapper Dan, and Maurice met to hear Lustig's plan; the business that brought him to Paris this time. Tony was assigned to make all the arrangements. He found a house in which they could meet. The owners were in America and were delighted to lease their home during their absence. The four men met to hear the plan. Lustig always worked slowly and divulged his plan step by step. At first they were told only to scan the Paris papers to find the names of salvage dealers, their location and what they could find out about their private lives and their business successes. Finally, after several meetings, he scaled the names down to four. Four good 'marks' he told them.

In the meantime, Roberta had contacted Victor's father and told him about the kidnapping. The older Lustig went to Paris himself to find his granddaughter and send her back to her mother. He found her in the Hotel Crillon early one morning and carried her out of the hotel himself and took her home with him. After a few days, he hired a Swiss maid to take her back to her mother.

Betty was enjoying her time in the hotel because she was seeing her father often. She didn't like that man that was with her mother now and she would have liked to stay in the hotel with her French maid. But, she loved being with her grandfather too, so she had to be spirited away again to be sent back to her mother. Victor was probably not as disturbed as he might have been, for business at the moment was taking all his time.

The four 'marks' who had been selected received hand-delivered invitations to meet at the house Lustig and his friends were occupying. According to a note found many years later among Roberta's things, the names of the four marks were: Armand Petain, Andre Maritan, Jacques Reynaud and Pierre Mayaud. Each of the four planners had been given one of the four marks to investigate thoroughly, so that Lustig knew all about each one when he arrived.

Lustig knew that they would have to appear official to the four marks, so Dan, of French descent and with fluent French-speaking ability, was instructed to get a date with a girl who worked in a government office. He was instructed to get a letterhead and the premiere's signature. Dan got a letterhead, but no envelope. Lustig then called his forger friend, 'Claude' at Rheims, and asked him to come in and meet them. He showed 'Claude' what he wanted and he returned in a few days with the letterhead, signature on the invitation, and all papers that were necessary to appear official.

The four marks came in special automobiles that were sent to bring them, hardly able to contain themselves to know why they were invited to a meeting by the premiere himself. Lustig told them that it was a state secret and they must not divulge what they would hear that day to anyone.

They were served an elegant dinner, using the owner's servants and dinner service with Lustig's food, wine and beer. Victor figured that the men he had invited to the dinner were more likely beer drinkers than wine drinkers. After the dinner he made the grand announcement: The government had decided to demolish the Eiffel Tower and would sell it to the highest bidder.

"Have your bids at my hotel by Monday morning," he told them. One of the men asked why the hotel and not at the government offices. Lustig squirmed interiorly. Were they getting suspicious? But he had an answer and it seemed to satisfy the questioner.

"To avoid publicity. Because of the nature of the act and the absolute necessity of secrecy. It would be much better at the hotel and not at an office where too many people might find out what was happening." The explanation seemed to satisfy all present.

The bids arrived promptly Monday morning, again brought by special cars provided by Tony. Lustig had already picked Jaques Reynaud as the one to whom he would sell the tower. On Tuesday morning, Dapper Dan called upon Monsieur Reynaud and told him that his bid was considered the best one and if he could produce the funds, the Eiffel Tower would be his to dismantle and sell to his own great advantage. Reynaud asked for a few days to negotiate the funds. He might have to sell some of his property to manage the ready cash. The following Monday morning, Monsieur Reynaud came to Lustig's hotel early. Victor had refused to be disturbed by the time the mark was taking. 'Give a mark all the time he wants, as soon as you have convinced him, that he wants to give his money.'

Lustig had a time table worked out to take effect after the mark appeared: thirty minutes to conclude the deal with Reynaud and receive his certified check from him; about the same amount of time to go to a bank and cash the check. Half of which he sent to Roberta in Kansas City and the other half which he divided equally among the four accomplices. Roberta never knew exactly how much he had sold the Tower for.

Then, there was a quick walk around the corner, where Tony and Dapper Dan awaited him with an automobile and they were off for a holiday in Vienna. After a month enjoying the best of Vienna society and watching the French newspapers for news that never leaked, they left for America again.

TWELVE

B UT IT WAS a sad homecoming for Victor. His Bertie was gone, married to another man; his father had thwarted him in taking his child away from him and returning her to her mother. Life was hard on him when he didn't have Bertie to constantly warn him, to tell him when to go ahead and when to hold back. He grew careless and was arrested three times in succession. There were no convictions, for he always managed to pay his way out, either from jail in the form of a fake escape, or before he ever got to jail.

One scheme which he did pull off successfully was to outsmart Al Capone. He asked his friend, Arnold Rothstein, to make an appointment for him with Capone. Arnie was a gambling friend of Victor. His personal life aside, he was considered the best person to make the appointment.

"What does he want?" Capone asked Arnie.

"I don't know. He just wants to meet you."

This was true. Lustig hadn't made up his mind what excuse he would use to meet Capone. Capone made the appointment for two weeks ahead and then changed it to three days. Lustig didn't have time to locate a mark or a project, so he just went to Capone, trusting that his native ingenuity would find him some excuse.

He went to Capone, jauntily carrying his walking stick. He submitted to the frisking which Capone's guards imposed upon him before he was admitted to the chief's presence. He entered and the big, lumbering Al Capone glared at his visitor.

"What ya want?" Capone growled at him.

Lustig, just as jauntily as his entrance had been, unscrewed the top of his walking stick and displayed a flask. Capone was interested. He brought two glasses and they toasted each other. Capone was beginning to admire the guts of this man. He eyed the walking stick again.

"That's quite an idea. My men never thought of frisking your walking stick. I'll have to tell them about this."

Roberta's diary doesn't tell what the scheme was that Victor soon thought up when he was in Capone's presence. But there was an exchange of money, a large amount, something around $100,000, which Lustig said he would double. It might have been a second sale of the Eiffel Tower. Lustig departed, promising to return as soon as the plan worked out.

Two weeks later he came back to Capone and returned the original money to him. "My business deal didn't work out, so I am returning your money to you." Lustig told him as he put the bills on the table in front of the big underworld figure. Capone's jaws fell open. Never before in his life had anyone returned money to him. This is all Roberta's journal had about the deal except that she said Victor always felt that he had pulled a trick on the king of crooks.

Back in Kansas City, Roberta was restless. She missed Vic and worried about him. Her jealousy, too, asserted itself. Vic was too attractive not to be attracting other women. And now that he was free, there was no limit to her imaginations. She still considered him hers. No other woman could ever claim him. Thus her days went on and she soon divorced Charles Gibson.

One day when she was driving along the street with Betty in the back seat, the child cried out, "There comes daddy."

At the moment Roberta was consumed with jealousy. She had heard that Victor was seen with other women and she could feel only jealousy that he was free to see them. At her child's exclamation, she looked up and saw that he was crossing a sidewalk in front of them. She shifted gears with a grinding sound and roared head on toward him in 'bull and matador' fashion. He, like the 'matador', stepped aside just in time. Then he turned and fled, coat tails flying, leading her on a mad and wild chase; she following with all the haste of the Packard she was driving.

"Mother, why are you chasing Daddy?" the child was screaming from behind her.

"Keep still. We're playing tag!"

"Why are you playing tag with Daddy? I want my Daddy."

"Sit down and keep still."

Just then the fugitive turned into a narrow alley. She followed and plunged into the alley. Two brick buildings loomed up before her. The wide Packard came to a grinding stop, wedged completely between the two buildings.

Victor, some 50 feet away, came over to the wedged-in car, opened the door and slipped into the seat beside her. He put his arms around her and Betty hugged them both from behind.

They were remarried August 4, 1925. This union lasted seven years. Victor Lustig loved his wife and would always love her, but he loved the life he had chosen to make for himself too. No matter what his past broken promises, he could not see why Roberta, his Buckle, could not go along with him just as willingly now as she had done at the beginning.

He thought of how, after every escapade, he would move quickly and go home to Roberta to rest a few days. Home was wherever they happened to be, in an apartment or in a hotel. He had always tolerated his wife's desire for a home, which was dangerous to his profession, but which always gave him a place to go. She had a hold on him that he could not explain.

After the remarriage, they went to Detroit. Roberta always had their furniture shipped to their destination if it was to be at least three months. All their statues, lamps, china, furniture, Betty's toys, as well as the large pieces of furniture, regardless of the expense, had criss-crossed the country many times.

In these years they were together, she moved into a large duplex in Detroit. She moved their furniture to the second floor and furnished the downstairs for Grace, the nurse and maid. Victor considered it was necessary. He never wanted to leave them alone for any length of time. He would be with them in the same hotel down the hall or in a hotel close by.

Roberta wanted to stay at least a year in Detroit and give her daughter a chance for a full year of school. No more intermittent tutors. Victor went to Paris after they moved to Detroit but he sent them post cards every day and boxes weekly with gifts for them all. When he came back that time, he went to the duplex and rested for two days in his favorite bathrobe, which Roberta always kept ready for him. He enjoyed some German beer and a little wine, but never any liquor. He didn't drink and couldn't tolerate drunks. He never allowed profanity around his wife and daughter, and vulgarity was not allowed in her presence. He loved her so much and had so much respect for her.

The third day at home was always the beginning of happy times. He was rested and Roberta would always have a sparkle in her eyes. He could never be unfaithful to her. That he had promised himself, there in Detroit.

He taught Betty the Morse Code. They would tap messages to each other on the palms of their hands.

She would tap out on her Daddy's hand: . . . (I love you, Daddy.) and he would return the message to her. More importantly, and often, he used their secret means of communication to admonish her when company was present and he feared what the child might say! . . . (Do not talk.) . . .or . . . (Go to your room.). All she needed was the pressure on her hand and she obeyed immediately.

He heard all about school in Detroit and followed her progress there.

Betty found school different but she liked it. However, there was one thing that bothered her. All of her school mates talked about their brothers and sisters. They had mothers at home cooking dinner and they complained that they had all the chores to do when they got home. Betty wanted to complain too. So, she told how her four brothers and three sisters were so lazy. They would do nothing and she had to do all the chores after she went home from school. She had to make the beds, wash the dishes and do a dozen odd jobs. She told how her four brothers and three sisters would do nothing and she had to do all the work when she got home. She also said that her father was a milk man. He worked all night and slept all day. That was why nobody saw him.

When her mother was asked to fill out some forms for the school records, the little fabrications came to light. Roberta explained that the child was lonely, that her father was away on business all the time and that she had always wanted brothers and sisters. She never mentioned to Betty that she knew about it, but she continued to caution her not to talk about her family in any way.

As Victor recalled this story about his child at school, did he by any chance feel any pangs of remorse that he would never be able to give her real home life? No matter how much her mother tried to make a home?

The school year had scarcely closed when they left Detroit to go to Texas. They would visit their friend Herschel Gray. But Victor's real reason for going to Texas was to find a man, a Texas sheriff who owned a haberdashery in Peoria, Illinois.

He remarked to Herschel soon after their arrival:

"I met a guy from Amarillo I'd like to go to see while I am here. He's a sheriff in some little berg outside of Amarillo."

"Yes, I've heard of him," Herschel replied. "He's involved in most of the activities of the town. Besides being sheriff, he's probate 'Judge' and has quite a marriage mill going. He owns most of the businesses in the town, some pretty shady, I'd guess."

"Yes, any sheriff who owns a haberdashery in Illinois and carried a club in Texas must be a little shady. You're right, he's involved in everything, even a madam."

Victor laughed. "He invited me down and said he would supply the 'party girls.' I told him I wasn't interested, but I would like to meet him again."

"I hear he's in pretty deep with that haberdashery. It's a little over his head. He's trying to bring it all to Amarillo and make up for his losses in Peoria," Herschel volunteered further information about the Texas sheriff.

Victor knew he had a mark then, so he told Roberta the next morning that they'd be going to Amarillo. To prepare for the trip, he purchased two identical suit cases. He filled one with Liberty Bonds and the other with blank paper.

Arriving in the Amarillo suburb, he found the sheriff and reintroduced himself as 'Count Lustig'. Their reunion was full of loud guffawas and plenty of liquor. Victor went along with it all, avoiding the drinks as much as he could and brushing off the guffaws. He slowly got around to a more serious subject.

"Do you know what I've got in this suitcase?" He was carrying the suit case with the Liberty Bonds.

"Your clothes, of course. Those fine ones you bought from me in Peoria. But come on to my store here tomorrow and see what I've got. I'm sure you'll want some of my handsome outfits."

"No, I don't have clothes in this bag. And I can't come into your shop to buy anything, for I must admit, I don't have the ready cash I had when I was in Peoria. Mr. Jones, I've got Liberty Bonds in this suit case. My father over in Zurich wanted to give me something substantial, he said. My father is not pleased with my way of living and thinks I spend money foolishly. That's why he invested in Liberty Bonds for me, something, he thought I could not throw away foolishly. Now, I know he wouldn't agree with me, but I'm terribly in need of cash. The Liberty Bonds in this bag are worth $80,000, I'd be willing to give them to you or any other buyer for $60,000."

Sheriff Jones saw the $20,000 offered him out of a blue sky, it seemed, and grasped it at once.

"Sell them to me, Count. I can use that extra $20,000 as slick as a whistle."

Victor opened the bag and showed him the packet of bonds, flipping through them to show that there was really $80,000 worth.

"Give me until tomorrow noon and I'll have the $60,000 for you."

"Fine."

"That's all, just give me a chance to go to the bank and make sure they can be redeemed at once. All you'll have to do then will be go to the bank and get your $80,000."

They parted, Sheriff Jones to go to the county money at his disposal and Victor to his hotel to spend a quiet evening with Roberta and Betty. The next day at noon he appeared at the sheriff's office, carrying the suit case that contained the blank pieces of paper. Tony was guarding the other suit case in the Rolls Royce with Roberta and Betty in it, ready to take off at once.

Lustig entered the sheriff's office and held out the suit case but grasping it firmly.

"Are you ready for the exchange?" Victor called out smiling. Sheriff Jones produced a roll of bills and took the suit case in exchange.

"Thanks, Sheriff, shall we meet again?" He walked out of the sheriff's office, restraining a more rapid exit and went directly to the Rolls, climbed in beside Tony, and they were off for Kansas.

THIRTEEN

PREVIOUS TO THE remarriage, Victor Lustig had wintered in Palm Beach, in 1925. He was alone and divorced from Roberta, who was married to Charles Gibson. But he was trying to win her back, so he purchased a mansion for her in the plush Palm Beach social area. He did win her back before the year was up and brought her to Florida, leaving Betty in Kansas with relatives. Roberta loved the palatial house with its indoor swimming pool that you could enter from the living room and swim under a wall into the pool room. "But it was like the apartment in New York," Roberta wrote in her diary, "used only a few months every few years." The Florida house was occupied only two months of the two-year ownership.

Victor had come to Palm Beach to make money. There was money in Florida, where all the rich and near-rich wintered, and Lustig wanted his share of it. In the white Rolls with a Philipino chauffeur (Tony and Grace were in New York with Roberta and Betty), he made his entrance into Palm Beach on a sunny afternoon. The chauffeur in white uniform opened the door of the Rolls and a handsome, well-dressed man, with a monocle in one eye, emerged in the presence of all the rich mothers who had eligible daughters. He went to his hotel room and little was seen of him for the next few days. That was his practice. Never hurry. Any deal was worth all the time he could give it. Finally, he began to appear on the beach in the afternoon, but still kept to himself. In the afternoon one day, his chauffeur appeared with a telegram in his hand. Lustig took it casually, in the presence of all the gaping eyes, looked at it and stuffed it in his pocket. Within an hour, another appearance of the chauffeur and another telegram. They continued until eight had been handed to him. The next day, he followed the same procedure. By the third afternoon, the telegrams were coming so fast that he did not bother to more than glance at them and stuff them in his pocket. Finally, he began to appear in the dining room and let himself become the focus of all eyes. He let it be known that the telegrams and cablegrams were from financiers who wanted to do business with him. The mothers of eligible daughters thought there was nobody like this handsome, mysterious man who had let it be known casually that he was a 'Count',

'Count Von Kessler', whose business interests took him all over Europe. The word count was enough to make some of the daughters' hearts flutter now and every mother was calling herself the mother of a countess.

But Victor Lustig was not looking for a wife; he was looking for a mark in this 'jet set' of socialites. It wouldn't be one who had already made it, he knew, not a Vanderbilt or a Whitney or a Carnegie or a Rockefeller, but one who had not 'made it' but was aspiring to social prestige.

Herman Loller was also wintering in Florida. Before the war, he had been a mechanic in New Jersey but he became rich making automobile parts during the war. After the war, he put his labors on the Maxwell automobile and planned to continue getting rich making Maxwells. He hadn't counted on a change in public taste, and when the Maxwell lost its prestige, Herman Loller feared losing his as well. He thought to regain his prestige not by going back to his mechanic shop and starting over, but by getting an 'in' with the rich in Florida. His wife was in Europe and his son and daughter in school, so he was living high in Palm Beach with two girl friends and showing off his boat in which he offered to take every one riding. But now his wife was returning in time for the holidays and he needed money as well as anonymity. Lustig had studied him and decided he was his mark. He got to know him and had many interesting conversations in which Loller confided his predicament and his need for money. He was amazed at 'Von Kessler's' show of money.

"How did you get it?" he asked.

Gradually, Victor told him about the money box, 'the only one in existence,' he said, carefully guarding it.

"I couldn't give this up for any amount of money. You see what it has done for me."

"But couldn't you sell it to me and make another one for yourself?"

"I don't think it would be good to have two such boxes," Victor said, "however I know all the specifications."

"Then sell it to me and make yourself another one. I'll give you $25,000 for it."

"That's not enough, but if it's all you can raise, I'll sell it to you at a sacrifice. I hope it will help you out."

Greedily, Loller handed over the $25,000 and took the magic box. Victor took the money and immediately left Palm Beach, Florida. He had $25,000 in his pocket, $21,000 of which was profit and, in six days of work, he had another box waiting for the next mark.

He waited a reasonable length of time and went back to Florida. He knew there was potential for money there and he wanted another try at it. This time he took Roberta with him to live in their palatial home. They had remarried and he looked forward to a happy home life again. Betty was in Kansas with her grandmother and aunts. The world did not yet know that he had a wife and daughter, so he checked in at Hotel Thomas in Gainsville.

Donald Rogers was in Palm Beach at the same time. He was on a business trip but had met a starlet from Hollywood and was having his affair with her; pending a divorce from his wife, he told 'Lily', the unsuspecting starlet. He had business in Havana and took Victor, whom he had met, Emil, Lustig's brother, and Lily, with him. Emil had become interested in Lily also and was content to amuse her when Donald Rogers was not around. Rogers confided to Victor that he was concerned about his affair with Lily, for his wife was coming to Palm Beach. He didn't know how he could lie out of this affair to her, for he feared Lily would squeal on him. He managed to leave Lily in Havana with a Cuban boy friend to look after her. When Rogers' wife arrived, he appealed to Victor to help him. Victor promised to do what he could and because of this concern, Rogers became easy bait for the money box. He was interested in anything that made money for him. Lustig soon sold him the magic box and he, Tony, Roberta and Emil left for New York and then to Kansas for Betty and Grace.

Rogers, when he found out he had been duped, went to the police and told the whole story, but from a different angle. It was Victor who had the affair with Lily. But Lily had vanished. No charges were ever filed and it was supposed that Rogers had sent her back to Hollywood.

This ended Lustig's two adventures in luscious, money-filled Florida, but he considered it worthwhile, for he was two money boxes poorer and $30,000 richer.

With these riches, he took his wife and daughter to Europe again. They went to Paris, London and Zurich to visit with Grandfather Lustig. It was the last time Betty would see him, the last time for a faint hope to spring up in the heart of a proud, old man for a son or a grand-daughter to succeed him.

Paris was always their best-loved spot. Victor loved it because much of his 'business' originated there; Roberta and Betty loved it because of the shopping for pretty clothes and the trips they took to the Eiffel tower to look down on the little people below. Betty loved feeling secure in the warm clasp of her mother's hand while her mother was feeling most insecure in the world of little people in which she was living. The year in Detroit had given her a taste of home life, which she so wanted.

They left Cherbourg on the Mauretania, May 4, 1927, to return home. Victor was traveling as 'Baron Frederick Von Kessler'. Roberta was traveling as Roberta Lustig with her small daughter, Betty Jean Lustig. They had adjoining cabins and were ready to settle down and relax on this, their favorite ship. The Titanic had become a forgotten fear to most travelers and there should have been nothing to distract the Lustig family, separated by day, united by night, from a peaceful trip home. But Victor could not feel complete ease. He was concerned. He knew the police had a 'want' out for him in New York and without a doubt, there could be a problem.

He decided the best direction to take was to announce his arrival as if nothing were wrong. So, he cabled the resident agent of the Secret Service in New York the date of his arrival and that he had urgent and valuable information for him. He signed the cable Count Victor Lustig, although he was traveling as Von Kessler.

Victor was not yet into counterfeiting, but the Secret Service assumed that was the valuable information he had for them, since their primary job at the time was to protect the currency.

Peter Rubano, resident agent in New York, read the cable and jumped to attention. Was this what they were looking for? He must not let Lustig elude him now after committing himself of his own volition. He contacted his chief assistant and the two men went immediately down to the ship's landing. They crossed out to the Mauratania in a pilot boat and walked confidently into Lustig's stateroom. "Secret Service," Rubano said carefully and looked around as though he expected his would-be captive to bolt and run.

Lustig was not prepared for this sudden invasion of his cabin and knew he would have to trust his ingenuity to handle Rubano. He had not yet collected his 'valuable information'. He had expected to talk to him in his office after his arrival, so he said at once: "We can't talk here. An interruption would destroy everything. We will have to wait and talk in your office."

But Victor had a reason for not wanting to escape the clutches of the Secret Service just yet. He was bringing back with him four large diamonds hidden in the heels of his shoes, two in each shoe. This hiding place for smugglers was known to customs and Victor was wondering how he could get past the customs without his loot being discovered. Quick thinking told him that Rubano and his assistant could get him by customs.

"It's going to take some time to get through customs," he said easily. "If we could get past there, I could go with you immediately to your office and give you the 'valuable information' I have for you."

"No problem there," Rubano told him. "I can see to that."

Thus the three walked freely out of the ship, Rubano flashing his Secret Service badge and Victor touching lightly his wife's shoulder and his daughter's head as he passed them. Roberta knew what that meant. He would see them soon and they should be silent. Customs seemed to know what it meant too, and with no waste of time, they were soon in Rubano's office.

Victor now began, ad libitum, to tell Rubano one story after another, all about people in Paris.

"I ran into a forger there. I thought you would need to know about him. His name is Henri Renard and his secret address is 11 rue Olivant. Then, there is a swindler I ran into, Monsieur Petard. If you investigate him a bit, I think you can get some valuable information. His address is 9 rue Farrar. On and on he went, naming one non-existent person after another. He described a cellar, a print shop and a swindler's den, all of them in Paris.

Peter Rubano listened for a while to all this useless information. What could he do? He had found nothing for which he could hold this wanted man. Finally, he stopped the speaker, saying casually, "If you think of anything else, be in touch."

'Count' Lustig apologized for taking up his time and stepped out on the sidewalk, used his handkerchief as his signal and walked one block west. A black limousine slithered by the curb and stopped. Tony, always waiting and always knowing what his master wanted, had followed him off ship and was waiting for him.

Victor stepped in, drew the shades and settled down for forty winks during the ride home to his wife and daughter. Roberta and Betty, after clearing customs, had hailed a taxi and gone immediately to what was home in New York, that first apartment they had furnished after their return from their honeymoon in Europe.

Roberta had been disturbed at the length of time it took Victor to clear himself this time and wondered if he was slipping. Betty had kept crying out anxiously for her daddy ever since he had touched the top of her head when he left the ship. "When will my daddy come back?" she asked. He came at last, had a hot bath and a shave, taking off his mustache, which was part of his disguise as 'Baron' Von Kessler, and became Victor Lustig again. 'Count' Victor Lustig, who was happy with his wife and daughter and proud that he had 'out-foxed a fox' again, when Peter Rubano fell under his spell.

FOURTEEN

THEY WERE DINING in the restaurant of the Book-Cadillac in Detroit. Victor, Roberta, Emil and his wife, Louise, Tom Kearney, Nicky Arnstein, Dapper Dan Collins, and Jack (Legs) Diamond. In ties and tails, furs and jewels, they were a handsome looking group, passing for high society diners.

Jack Diamond was tall, thin and handsome. Dapper Dan was a woman's darling: tall, handsome and blond; Tom Kearney was the fine looking business man; Nicky Arnstein, handsome and charming at all times. Roberta's red-gold glory always made her and Victor a striking couple and Emil and Louise added their part nobly. They were the cynosure of all eyes that night as they sat at their table and reminisced about the past. They talked in low voices, for their past was not always 'high society' but it was jovial, the memories of people who were pleased with themselves, albeit not always a 'legal' pleasure.

Roberta added spice to the conversation which was revolving around baseball, golf tournaments and the World Series. Finally, they got to the Chicago White Sox and Roberta interposed naively, "Did the White Sox make many touchdowns?"

There was a moment's silence at the table. Vic closed his eyes as was his habit when in shock and clenched his teeth.

"Buckle, baseball is home runs and football is touchdowns."

"But, Vic, I thought as long as they got to the other side it was either."

Finally, the diners could hold out no longer and broke into hysterical laughter, while Roberta retreated behind her jewels.

"I'll take her bet any day." Tom Kearney said wiping his eyes of tears from laughter. Jack came to her rescue. "Roberta, ignore those crazy people. You'll learn if Vic will take time to teach you. You've taught him a few things."

"Talking about the White Sox, remember the 'fix' in the 1919 world series?" Nicky Arnstein interposed to get the conversation off Roberta's back.

"Remember it?" they all cried out. "You're the one who should remember it, Nick, you almost got pulled into it!"

"I was an innocent man and I know nothing about the 'fix'.

"What was it?" Victor asked. "I never heard of a 'fix' of the Series."

"You didn't and still you knew all about Arnold Rothstein. Arnie 'fixed' the 1919 World Series." He always denied it but everyone knew he supplied the green. The players did the 'fix'.

"And do you remember what Fannie said when she heard that you did the 'fix'? She said Nicky 'fixed' the World Series. Why, he couldn't fix an electric light bulb in a socket!"

This brought another laugh from the group and then they realized that a gentleman and a lady were standing at the table.

"Excuse me, gentlemen. But I overheard your conversation and recognized the name of a gangster. I am Steve Stone and this is my wife, Greta."

The Stones were invited to join the table and drinks were ordered. When Victor Lustig drank he always became sleepy. If there was no opportunity to take a nap, he couldn't keep from dozing wherever he was, though never sleeping enough to miss the conversation and waking up long enough to answer any question put to him.

Lustig's guests, of course, were wondering how long before Vic would take this mark and by what means: money box, bonds, bank opening or race track. But Emil, at an opportune moment, had whispered to Victor, "This sucker is mine." Victor didn't always trust his brother to carry through a deal but he was too sleepy to care now and decided to let him go ahead. He had introduced his brother as Fritz von Kemph and he heard him now making a luncheon date with Steve Stone.

That night Emil discussed his strategy with his brother. He wanted to use the 'silver mine' caper which Victor had used before. He had all the documents, letter heads, and cancelled envelopes. All that was needed was for Emil, the master forger, to insert the postage date to two weeks prior to the present date.

The letter read that a 'Mr. Stewart Gross' had lost considerable money playing poker and wished to sell his interest in a silver mine in Silver City, Colorado. He was begging 'Count' Lustig to purchase the mine under an agreement that he would sell it back to Gross when the latter was able to redeem it. He feared, if 'Count' Lustig would not come to his rescue, that he would have to sell to some speculators and would never get his mine back. The contract would involve some $80,000 with a 5% interest on any unpaid balance. It stated that the 'silver mines' were well known by investors as blue ribbon.

At the luncheon the next day, Emil (or 'Fritz') first talked to Stone about the wealth of 'Count' Victor Lustig and his stupidity. He would never be able to buy the silver mines on the terms of the contract. Then he showed his guest the documents. Stone read them over avidly and said at once he wanted in on this fantastic deal, but how was the question. Emil suggested that they both think about it, but Stone insisted that he was ready to act immediately. 'Fritz' didn't know whether his stupid friend would let him buy the mines or not since they had been offered to him. 'Fritz' said he would see what he could do with him.

"How much do you want to negotiate this deal for me?" Stone asked.

Emil told him $10,000 would be fine. When he told his brother about the plan and the fact that the victim wanted to pay $80,000 for the mines and was giving him $10,000 for playing the middle man in the deal, Victor glared at him.

"You fool! You always think in nickels. You should have asked for $25,000 or no deal. Don't you know that any mark willing to pay $10,000 would just as willingly pay $25,000?"

"I'll go back and tell him I want $50,000," Emil said.

"No, do it right the first time or not at all."

Emil set up an appointment with Stone and an attorney, a Mr. Weisman, who had become an alcoholic and lost his license. The disbarred lawyer sobered up enough to 'represent' Mr. Gross in closing the deal and would get $500 out of it. Mr. Weisman, who was really Charlie Little, a friend of Emil, played the part to the hilt, insisting that the party to the second part should be Victor Lustig, but since 'Count' Lustig didn't need the money that the mine would bring in, he was willing to let Stone be the buyer.

Stone opened his bag and revealed $80,000 in U.S. currency. He departed with the contract and walked away quickly to join Mrs. Stone and leave for Albany at once. Everyone else scattered too. Grace had Betty and the dog and was on a train bound for Chicago. Victor and Roberta met Tony and were off too, to Chicago.

Repercussions were tremendous. Stephen Stone soon learned that there was no Mr. Gross and no silver mine that would be bought for $80,000. Police had advised him that 'Fritz' and Victor were brothers. He began investigations in every large city of the United States. The newspapers carried the story of Stephen Stone and his crusade in which he spent thousands of dollars to track down the $90,000 he had originally lost, ten of it to Emil for his help as middle-man.

One New York paper had the lead 'The relentless Stephen Stone still searches every major city in the United States for Emil and Victor Lustig'.

The Lustig family never went back to Detroit again and their guests that night no longer stayed at the Book-Cadillac, for fear Stone's investigators would be watching there.

But the whole affair meant almost tragedy to the Lustig family. No longer could they enjoy a fully relaxed stay in any place. It was like a plague that had entrapped Victor, Roberta, Tony, Grace and Betty. They were always on the alert. The shadow of Stone was always before them, even if the man not there. He began a 'Catch the Count' campaign in every major city and Victor had to reduce his income by one half, in pay-off to the police, to keep out of the Stone clutches. Had it not been for police who were alerted and given a pay-off, Stone would have found him in less than six months after he 'bought' the silver mine.

Victor took his family to Colorado shortly after the Stone swindle in Detroit. He sold another silver mine in its home state for $20,000. He sent Roberta and Betty on ahead and went back to his hotel room via the service elevator to get his things and meet Tony to leave town immediately. The elevator boy who took him up remarked on letting him off, "The police chief was down at the front desk as I came through the lobby." Victor stiffened at once. He took a handful of bills out of his pocket and handed them to the boy.

"Don't tell anyone you brought me up."

The boy grinned, "No sir, no sir, thank you sir."

He strolled back through the lobby as the police chief was leaving the desk. The latter saw the boy counting bills in his hand and rightly guessed that Victor Lustig was around. Stone's alert had clicked.

The Chief of Police made a forced entry into the suspect's hotel room and found Lustig with one foot out of a window ready for a hasty exit after the elevator boy's warning. Chief Martin arrested Lustig, handcuffed him and escorted him down the service elevator to an unmarked car waiting in the alley. He put Lustig in the seat beside him and threw the suit case in the back seat. As they drove through a lonely street in a residential area, the chief began to talk quietly.

"I'm sure, 'Count' Lustig, that you think I am a small-town fella with no brains and you can whitewash your way out of this, but I'll tell you right off of the top of my hat, my friend, there's a Stone fella that has blood in his eye for you. I met Stone, 'Count Victor Lustig', and you'd better thank your stars that it was me coming through that door and not Stone."

"I'm a man of few words and little savings – I have a family and I don't intend to sit by watching all the other guys making money saving your neck and I wind up with empty pockets. You've been up to something here in this town and I don't care what – I just want a piece of the action and I'll make no bones about it and don't think you can smooth-talk your way out of this, Mr. 'Count', not with me. So make an offer and it had better be a good one, better than any Stone is offering."

Victor couldn't help but admire the man for his out-spoken challenge, but he was chagrined at the turn things had taken. He remained silent, trying to make mental note of his pay-off abilities. He had $10,000 in his wallet and his secret pockets and there was $20,000 in the suit case in the back of the car, netted that morning with the sale of a silver mine.

Martin pulled the car over near a vacant lot and sat strumming his fingers over the steering wheel, puffing on a fresh cigar he lit with great care. Each move he made now was quiet, deliberate and had a note marked, 'final'.

"Chief," Victor's calm and equally deliberate tone broke the silence, "I'm at a loss and will not try to avoid the facts. You have me and you know I am not violent, don't you?"

"Yes, I know that."

"Then please remove the handcuffs."

Martin removed a key from his vest pocket, unlocked the cuffs and dropped them on the seat between them, still puffing on his cigar. Victor then realized that this man was determined and could as easily lock him up as free him.

Then Martin broke the silence. "Talk, Lustig, let's hear it. Where is it, on you, or in that suit case back there?"

Lustig looked back at the suit case, reached his arm back but it was too far for him to reach it. He started to open the door and get out to get the bag.

"Hold it, Lustig," Martin interposed quickly, yanking the cigar out of his mouth. "I'll get it."

By now, Victor realized that the quiet calmness of the Chief of Police could not be equated with his alertness. The man was indeed determined and aware of Victor's reputation for escaping from far more hazardous encounters than this, and Victor knew that he could not escape or talk his way free today. Martin brought the case around to Victor, who turned and removed a cover. There it was, $20,000 in $500 bills.

The Chief of Police almost lost his composure.

"How much is it?" he asked breathlessly.

"$20,000," Lustig answered.

"I'll take it," he said as though fearing the $20,000 would rise and fly away.

That was all he asked for. The $10,000 on Lustig's person was safe.

"I'll drive you to a telephone," the chief said to Lustig as he closed the case, "and I want you to get out of town immediately."

"Can't you drive me to town?"

"No, just to a telephone, and I want you to be out of town in an hour."

"I could be out of town in 30 minutes if you drove me to town," he countered, but he knew it was useless. He realized that the Chief of Police did not want anyone to see him with Lustig, so from the telephone, the Chief drove on and Victor called Tony, who was there in a few minutes.

Vic was angry and silent.

"What happened?" Tony asked.

"I can't talk now. Just get me away as fast as you can."

Roberta recorded in her journal that her husband became very emotional every time he thought of the event. "$20,000!" he would scream out to her or to the listening walls. "All gone. All my hard work, gone – all because of that Stone. He'll never get me! Never! Never! He'll never find me."

And he didn't. Stone died in 1933, two years before the Secret Service caught 'Count' Victor Lustig.

FIFTEEN

BETTY WOULD WAKE in the middle of the night and hear a great bustling as they packed to go elsewhere. And she would know that they were moving again.

She once said: "I knew that I had to make friends quickly and would have to leave them just as quickly and never let my friends know where we were going. I wouldn't even have time to say goodbye, never write to them because of the fear that the law would learn of our whereabouts."

This night she heard the familiar bustling around. Her mother and the servants were packing. Her father was never there to help with the packing. He always had to leave early and tell them the meeting place where he would be. Many nights the maid would carry her in her nightgown to kiss him goodbye. This night she knew they were packing because the dog Togo was in her room. She and Togo would be the last ones to 'pack'. Once Togo had actually been packed when the dresser drawer in which she had been placed was closed and she was sent on with the dresser.

Togo was the family pet and went with them wherever they went. Victor, as well as everyone else, loved Togo. Once he had risked his life to rush out of the apartment in his shorts and socks, when Togo got out by mistake. He rushed down the crowded street to catch her and carry her back home. Had the police seen him and arrested him for appearing in public undressed, they would have found they had a bigger catch than a dog chaser.

Now Togo was in her basket in Betty's room. They would pack her room last. There was never any confusion about this packing. Every time they arrived at a new destination, they rented three garages, one of them was for the barrels, boxes, paper, crates, etc., in which they packed their furniture to ship ahead of them. The other two were for their cars. One piece of furniture that always went with them no matter where they went was the desk Victor had bought for Roberta shortly after Betty was born. Roberta once tried to count the number of times it had criss-crossed the country. 'It must have been at least 75 times,' she thought.

"Mother's day should be celebrated on the day the child is born," Victor always said. "That will always be my mother's day. Remember your mother daily, Skeezix," he would say to his little daughter, lapsing into his German speech, "because without your mudder, you vud'nt be here."

Grace was the faithful maid who took care of Betty and helped with the packing in the dead of night. She and Tony were always there to do it. They never complained, never asked where or why. Betty loved Grace and often told hotel attendants that she was her mother. Their smiles would be their only response, for Victor would have taken care of any doubts or discriminations by a generous sleight-of-hand gift.

This night Betty lay wide-eyed, listening to the soft movements of the busy packers. She didn't want to move that night. She had made a new little friend and didn't want to leave her. She got up and took the dog to bed with her and pulled the covers over her head.

Roberta finally came into her child's room. She talked quietly to her as she helped her dress and packed her suitcase, one large one and one small one. There were four large suit cases for Victor and Roberta, the dog's travel cage, all to be taken when Roberta and Betty left. Tony hailed a cab and placed the suit cases in it and gave the address of a vacant apartment.

When they arrived at the apartment, the driver placed the suit cases outside the door of the apartment, but Roberta did not open the door until he had left. She went in, dragging the suit cases after her and waited with Betty for less than an hour. Finally, there were three taps on the door. Roberta peeked out, said something and received the reply she was expecting. She opened the door to a uniformed chauffeur with a limousine waiting outside. Silently, he helped them out to the automobile and they started on their way. Everybody slept but Roberta and the driver. Betty slept on her mother's lap and Togo slept at Roberta's feet.

After they had traveled some time, Betty woke up and said she had to go to the bathroom. Roberta was prepared for that too. Betty and her mother got out of the car. Togo got out too and was frisking around. The highway patrol drove up to see what they were doing. Roberta appeared in view with a small square box with a round hole at the top and no bottom.

"My daughter had an emergency and we had to stop," Roberta told him. He looked at the contraption she had in her hand and felt that he couldn't contend with that statement and drove away.

In her haste, Roberta had placed a wool dress on Betty. The child cried and complained. The wool was itchy. She wouldn't wear it. Finally, her mother took her by the shoulders and faced her.

"Your father would have been in trouble if we had not left immediately. Your other dresses are packed and I cannot get to them. You are slowing us down and will cause trouble for your father."

Betty stopped crying at once. She would bear it for daddy, but not forever, she told herself.

They arrived at the train station in Chicago. They had driven from Detroit and Betty knew she would see Tony and the rest of the luggage in a few days. They went into the railroad station, where they were escorted into an office. Betty was placed in a chair and poor little Togo whined in her cage-prison. Roberta was in a full length mink coat and at once passed some money to the smiling railroad official.

Betty again announced, "I have to go to the bath room."

"I have a private bath room she can use," the railroad man said and led her to it. Like a flash, she had an idea. She went into the small lavatory, locked the door behind her, twisted and squirmed as she unbuttoned the wool dress, from the left shoulder, down the armhole, down to the waist and on to the hem, all cloth-covered buttons the size of a dime. She finally stepped out of the dress and stuffed it, the itchy dress with the itchy long sleeves down into the toilet stool and shut the lid on it. She put on her coat, buttoned it up carefully from hem to neck and stepped out of the private bathroom. They were escorted to the train by quite a detour, through a baggage room, around and between numerous parked railroad cars, and finally reached an empty train. That part of the train was apparently being pushed to join the other cars. The compartment was overheated and Betty wanted to take her coat off. She asked her mother where her dresses were. "The large suitcase was put in the baggage car by mistake," her mother told her and she would have to wear the dress she had on, whether it itched or not. Betty promptly took her coat off and stood jubilantly before her mother in her silk underslip.

Betty awoke the next morning to find her mother already dressed. She had secured the baggage during the night and had a dress ready for her child to put on. She left the compartment and told Betty to lock the door behind her. Betty lifted the shade of the window a bit to peek outside. There she saw Grace in a white nurse's uniform pushing a wheel chair. In it was her father. She recognized him and wasn't surprised at what she saw. She had seen many such curious scenes before when they were moving. He was in the wheel chair with his leg in a cast, his arm in a sling, a wool blanket wrapped around him and his head down on his chest with a felt hat pulled down to his ears. He was being lifted out of the wheel chair by Tony and a porter. Betty listened for the tap on the door from her mother and they carried her father in, the wheel chair following. They all worked together taking off his disguise after the porter had left. He grabbed his little girl with his one free arm.

"How's my little Skeezix?" and he held her tight. She held on tight to him and they didn't say another word. He was safe and his daughter was happy.

There were four compartments now, one for Tony, one for Grace, one for Victor and Roberta, and one for Betty. They had the entire section of the train and rode in it to California. Tony, Grace and Betty went to their meals. Victor and Roberta had theirs brought to them.

Victor's leg itched under the heavy cast which he still wore as a precaution and kept his arm in a sling when the porter was in the compartment. Betty told him about the wool dress episode and tried to comfort him when he said his leg itched. He had the cast taken off only after they reached California. There they stayed for two months in the home of a beautiful movie star on Pacific Coast Highway, Malibu. Tony, Grace and Togo stayed too in the servant's quarters. Victor stayed with his family. They all swam and enjoyed the great outdoors on the estate of the 'beautiful lady' as Betty called her. This was probably the longest time that Victor had been with his family and they were all very happy.

Roberta awoke to find Victor standing over her. "Get up and dress. We are going back to Kansas. I have business there and you can see your mother." Roberta hated to leave this beautiful place, this carefree time when there was no rush, no secrecy, just complete relaxation and easy conversation among them all; hosts and guests. But she would be glad to see 'Mama', so she was up, dressed and had Betty dressed by the time the hostess called them to breakfast.

They started out on their long trip to Kansas, Grace and Betty in the back seat of the car, Victor and Roberta in the front taking turns at driving. Tony was not with them. He had become ill; older age was approaching and the hurried life he was leading as the Lustigs' chauffeur, agent, arranger, and confidant, was taking its toll. He remained behind in the mild, health-giving climate of California. Victor eventually set him up in business, a restaurant. Tony married and with a faithful wife, lived long enough after Victor's death to fill Roberta and Betty in on details of that whirl-wind life which he had shared with them for a significant number of years.

Victor never had a driver's license and he was a horrible driver, so his wife had to watch him closely when he insisted on giving her rest periods from driving. Thus they arrived in Kansas, Roberta and Betty happy to see their family again and Victor ready to pull another mark out of his bag of researched miscreants, considering it a good deed to uncover their misdeeds.

But their happy days as a family were nearing an end, this time forever. After their remarriage, Roberta at first went every place with her husband. She was so fiercely jealous that she could not trust him out of her sight. She could never see him speaking to another woman without pain. She knew how attractive he was to women and she knew how much he liked the company of women; intelligent women who could carry on conversations with him. He had no use for emotional, stupid women who depended on their good looks to take them through their world of men. This attitude only increased Roberta's insecurity. She never knew where she could place herself in these catagories of women, so she resorted to jealousy as a shield.

In one year, 1926, they were in New York, Chicago, Detroit, Kansas City, Montreal, Boston, Paris, Cherbourg, Berlin, Munich, Naples, Spain and Italy, with Lustig running from the law and his wife chasing after him.

Finally, she gave up. Since they never traveled as husband and wife, she had a difficult time watching him, so she stayed at home to better care for her daughter, but stretching her jealous imagination to its limits. With Roberta staying at home in some hotel room in the United States with her daughter, Victor made many trips alone to Europe. On one of these trips he met Ruth Etting, a vaudeville singer, a part of the 'Ziegfeld Follies'. He loved music and Ruth, a singer, fascinated him. He saw her often. 'How could a man, who had so often vowed eternal love for his wife whom he really loved, have an affair with another woman?' Did he ask himself this question and go without an answer? Someone tried to explain it by saying he was like all European men who had one faithful wife and to whom they did not think themselves unfaithful because of their interest to other women.

When Victor's affair with Ruth Etting, more or less magnified, reached Roberta's ears, her jealousy rose to its highest pitch. This was the last. She filed for divorce the second time. She married Doug Conner, a man unworthy of her in every way, and Victor married Sue Miller in Chicago. Thus these two people, who would always love each other, let stubborness and jealousy lead them further apart at every step.

Years later, Betty sat staring at a newspaper clipping, 'Ruth Etting, film star, singer, dies.'

She read through the lead paragraph: 'Colorado Springs, Colorado (AP) – Ruth Etting Alderman, former film star and singer, has died at the age of 80.'

She didn't need to read on; to hear again about the song and film credits of this 'Ziegfeld Follies' girl, this 'radio show' girl, this 'film star' whose life had been made into a film, 'Love me or Leave Me', which could well have been her message to Victor Lustig long after he had loved her and left her.

'What an unsolved, contradictory man my father was,' she thought as the clipping fell from her hands. She closed her eyes and saw the whole panorama of his life.

His fascination for Ruth Etting, although brief, was strong. So was his fascination for the many people whose paths crossed his, his fascination for Jack (Legs) Diamond, an underworld character, and for an honest, respectable man like Tom Kearney, or for a long list of movie stars, politicians, servants like Tony and Grace, or collaborators in his own profession.

He asked much of his friends. They couldn't gossip or tell off-color jokes or disrespect women. These were his own traits and a 'friend' had to measure up. If he didn't, 'Count' Victor Lustig dropped him at once.

He felt sorry for Fanny Brice and tried to convince Nicky Arnstein that he should stay with her. He believed women should stand by their husbands even if the men had other women. He thought that was all right, but the women had to be faithful.

His daughter loved being with him, the two of them alone riding the merry-go-round; he behind her on the horse so he could watch her. She'd pass by the gold ring so he could get it and he pretended to be so pleased that he got a free ride.

He could win at chess but never at checkers. Her mother used to say checkers were too easy for him. Things had to be complicated before he would consider them worthy of his time. He loved to take watches apart and put them back together again. He loved the zoo and knew the names of all the unusual birds and animals, their habits and their habitats. The ordinary ones he would pass by.

He loved 'nuns' but had no use for 'priests'. He thought they pressured the nuns to do all the small jobs of the church. He hated to see the nuns in their long, hot habits. When he wanted to buy jewelry for Betty's favorite teacher, he was disappointed when told she could not wear it. He loved to go fishing and wear old clothes, although he was immaculate in his dress and often changed his white silk shirts several times a day. He liked to catch the fish but couldn't stand to bait the hook.

Betty picked up the news clipping and saw again Ruth Etting's name. But she didn't keep him. No one ever possessed him, not Ruth Etting, nor Roberta, nor Sue Miller, his second wife; not a prison nor even a rocky fortress. He was somehow outside of them all – an enigma that was never solved.

SIXTEEN

T HAT FIRST CHRISTMAS away from her daddy, Betty wrote later, was her saddest Christmas. Her father had always made Christmas so lovely and happy with a tree, crib set, and lots of love and good cheer, no matter where they were.

Now there was nothing but a hated step-father drinking with her mother. There was only one bright spot, a box from Uncle Jack. The gift had come early that Christmas, before Jack (Legs) Diamond was killed, December 16, 1931. It was a beautiful seal-skin coat and muff with a white ermine collar and cuffs. Betty was sitting by the side of the bed when her mother brought her Uncle Jack's present. She put the coat on and crawled under the covers. She thought about the goat Uncle Jack had given her a long time ago when she was just big enough to sit in the goat wagon and drive all around with Daddy or Mother close beside her, a loving hand on her shoulder. Uncle Jack bought the goat back in New Jersey and sent it in a horse trailer to Kansas City, where it was always kept for her special delight when they were there. She remembered how her mother called it the richest goat in the world because Uncle Jack had probably paid for it with some diamonds he had stolen.

Uncle Jack was always very special to Betty. She didn't know anything about 'Legs' and his dubious background or about the diamond heist in which 'Legs' stole $100,000 worth of diamonds that had just come in on the Aquitania simply by using two Cadillacs with five armed men in each car to block the truck that was transporting the diamond pouch.

Betty only knew that she loved the goat and loved Uncle Jack for sending it to her. She only saw the kind and good side of this potentially different kind of a man who, like Victor Lustig, took the 'wrong' road at some stage in his life. She remembered now, as she felt warm and soothed under the covers how, when she was four years old and leaving for her seventh trip to Zurich to see her grandfather Lustig, Uncle Jack arrived breathless just before they boarded the ship. He was carrying a large box for her. She opened it and saw a beautiful doll. It was four feet tall, too large for her to carry. Jack said, "One foot for every birthday you have had." He picked her up, sat her on his shoulders, swung her around and said:

"I'll wait for you, Princess, and when you grow up I will marry you."

He kissed her and stood waving at her when they left. Victor was furious when he saw what was happening. He saw to it that never again was 'Legs' Diamond seen with his family. But his gifts to Betty continued up to the seal-skin coat for the last holiday he would spend on earth.

With her Uncle Jack's coat on her under the covers on a bleak Christmas night, she fell asleep whispering.

"Please, God, let my mother and daddy be back like we were. Please, God, I promise I will be good."

She prayed that prayer every day until she was 16 years old. She finally stopped then, for it didn't work.

After Christmas, Roberta took Betty to Kansas. On the way, she told her that Uncle Jack was dead. The child burst into tears. She was planning to run away as soon as she would have a chance and go to Uncle Jack in New York. She knew his address and she would find him and ask him to find her daddy. She knew he would do it. Now that was all over.

After a few days with Uncle Paul and Aunt Ethel, her mother took her to a convent boarding school, where her father had arranged for her attendance to get her away from her hated step-father.

When Roberta put Betty in school, she told the nuns Betty's father would take care of her expenses. That he did. He visited her often and became a good friend of the mother superior, who spoke German and liked this young countryman of hers who had his daughter in their boarding school. Lustig liked her too. He said later that one person in the world to whom he would entrust his life was that mother superior. Trust it to her, he probably did. It is known, although it is not in the convent annals, that she harbored him some way one night and saved him from arrest.

Betty was happy during her four years in boarding school. It was her first regular school life, except for her one year in Detroit and with difficulty she learned to study and bring her grades up to a respectable mark. She rode her horse, Scarleg, in the school's riding program. She loved Scarleg and told her father she deserved a new wardrobe. She got it, a complete riding outfit the next time her father came to see her.

Used to luxury, she expected luxury even in her boarding school. She enjoyed all the privileges the school could offer. Every time her father went to Europe, she ordered him to bring back gifts for her class mates. He brought them expensive jewelry, everything she asked for. The florist and the candy store man in the town probably saw their best times while 'Count' Victor Lustig was their patron.

Then, one day, the bubble burst. The news broke that Victor Lustig, the biggest swindler and counterfeiter America had ever known, was apprehended. He was in

Chicago. Roberta had taken Betty on a little vacation from school and took her to see her father. Doug Conner, Roberta's husband, had always been jealous of his wife's first husband. He tracked her now to Chicago, found out where Lustig was and reported him to the Secret Service.

This time, Lustig made no effort to buy himself out of conviction. "He just gave up," Roberta noted in her journal. She wrote: "Vic was fed up, tired, and he just gave up. This time I wasn't in the wings as I had been in the past to go to friends or to go to a deposit box and withdraw enough money to assure his release. Police records show how many arrests, but they don't show how many times Vic paid off and they were not ever recorded as arrests. If Vic had not given up and screamed out 'guilty', they wouldn't have gotten him this time either. I should have been with him and he wouldn't have done that. That woman (meaning his second wife Sue Miller) didn't do her job. Vic would take chances and I would scream out at him and thrust the records in his face and stop him."

When they arrested him in Chicago, police found a key on him that opened a locker in a Times Square subway station in New York that contained $52,000 in counterfeit money.

Back in her boarding school, Betty's playmates formed a ring around her and sang: "Poor little rich girl, your father is a crook." These were the playmates who were wearing the expensive jewelry, bracelets and necklaces that Betty had asked her father to bring them from Paris; the same children who had enjoyed parties almost monthly and especially on holiday occasions, always paid for by her father. Now they were taunting her about her father, who had been apprehended as a crook. The child, not knowing what else to do, threw herself on the ground and cried in the grass. That was the only place for her, she felt, and she remained there, arms over her head, until a nun came running to stop the taunts and take the weeping child into the house with her.

SEVENTEEN

THE SECRET SERVICE of the United States has two duties: to guard the President and to guard the currency. In the early 1930's the country was so loaded with counterfeit money that the economy of the nation was threatened. New York, especially, was suffering from this surfeit of counterfeit money. Governor Lehman called on the Secret Service to begin work. Their search for several years finally resulted in the arrest of Victor Lustig, the king of counterfeiters.

By 1933 prohibition was out; bootlegging and speak-easies were dead, the country needed a new currency and Victor Lustig needed a new medium. Not that he had trafficked in bootlegging, but the money box had gone out with the prohibition era and he needed a new line.

By chance he met a man named William Watts when he was visiting some of Roberta's relatives in Hutchinson, Kansas. Watts and he entered into conversation and Lustig became interested.

"I'd like to contact you again, so when you get a permanent address, give it to my friend Tom Kearney in St. Louis. Tom will relay it to me."

Lustig gave Watts Kearney's address in St. Louis. It was several months before Tom notified him that he had an address for him. It was 295 Palisades, Union City, New Jersey, overlooking the Hudson River.

Roberta's diary is silent about Victor's relations with William Watts. She was divorced from him now and didn't know all of his intrigue. But Betty remembers three trips she made to Watts' apartment with her father. She remembers Watts as a nice man who lived alone, or at least no one appeared to be living with him when she and her father saw him. He loved good music and he and Victor exchanged music notes or listened to records together. Watts gave her a ring once with her name and a fleur-de-lis engraved on it.

On all three visits there were long conferences between the two men, while the little girl sat, watched the river and played with Watts' cat. Out of these 'conferences' was forged a partnership that gave Victor Lustig a new medium of swindling and which in the early 1930's flooded the financial market with so much counterfeit currency that the economy of the nation was threatened.

Watts, the master engraver, was happy to team up with one man, when Victor Lustig offered him the opportunity. He always feared leaks and the consequences when he was working with the people of the underworld. Too many people knew what was going on.

Lustig and Watts had plates for $100, $20 and $10 bills which poured out counterfeit money. Lustig was the distributor through underworld channels.

The Secret Service was hot on the trail of both Watts and Lustig, or rather, on the trail of the counterfeiters. Little by little they pieced together bits of evidence. They had heard of an engraver who made out in Chicago named William Watts. But he had dropped out of sight seven years before. They found a bit of evidence that Watts knew Victor Lustig, the great swindler and gambler who had been arrested some 80 times but never convicted. The Secret Service, however, had no power over him except in connection with the nation's currency. They must find him and convict him on that score.

After months of slow research, watching for a man who would correspond to the picture posted in every post office in the country, a group of Secret Service men were huddled on a street corner in New York. All clues had avoided them so far and they were wondering what to do next. Suddenly, one of them whispered to the others, "Look there." A Chevrolet was passing in front of them driven by a chauffeur. The car pulled to one side a half block down the street and parked. There was the man they were looking for. The head man immediately gave orders and they surrounded the car. One of the men opened the door of the Chevy and yelled "Secret Service", as he pulled the man from the car.

"What's this all about?" Lustig smiled at them and feigned innocence.

"You know what it's all about. You can answer later."

Roberta remarked later, "Victor knew better than to have his chauffeur drive him in a Chevrolet, anyone would notice such a stupid thing."

They spent the next 32 hours interrogating him and wearing him out. They let him go to the men's room only twice and then, under supervision. Lustig, with his genius mind, was far superior to these men of mediocre intelligence who had been trained in only one field, police work, and who possessed not one bit of Lustig's charm and powers of evasion. They gave him a sandwich and a cup of coffee once and kept up the interrogation. They knew their only chance of winning was in wearing him out. They also knew he required a lot of sleep. And wear him out they finally did.

"Do you know William Watts?" they asked him over and over. Finally, Lustig admitted a slight acquaintance with him. This was their first indention into the mystery that clouded the counterfeit currency that they were trying to solve. Their next task was to find out where Watts was and get the counterfeiting plates from him. This was their only chance of a conviction. To them, Watts was a much more important man than Victor Lustig. They finally realized that they could get no more information from him about Watts. All of the information they got came from a tired, sick and hungry man. Only small bits and pieces they would later piece together to eventually locate Watts. Never, did Victor Lustig inform on Watts. They sent Lustig to the New York Federal Prison to await his trial.

Lustig wasn't beaten yet. He put his ingenuity to work again, saved a sheet every time clean sheets were brought to him and made a rope of them which he kept concealed under the mattress of his bed. One day, while the guards were all at lunch, he induced a relief guard to open a window for him. Money that was originally concealed in the secret pockets of his trousers and suit coat had been cleverly transferred without detection to his prison clothing. This money paid off the guard. He stepped out, dropped down his sheet rope and tested its strength as he tied it to the window casing. Then, he started down with one free hand doing a window washing job. Pedestrians below looked up briefly at the 'window washer' and passed on their way. When the 'window washer' reached the ground, he bowed jauntily to the passersby, went around the corner of the building, still in prison garb and hailed a cab. Undetected, he went to his tailor, who outfitted him in civilian clothes. Newly outfitted he went to a deposit box, withdrew some money and left for the convent boarding school with it's 'friendly' mother superior to see his daughter.

The mother superior came to Betty. "You're daddy is here," she said, "but you must not tell any of the other children that he is here. Go to the chapel and wait there until I call you."

Betty seemed to understand. This is like it used to be, she thought. After a few days of harboring in an obscure town, he deemed that the Secret Service had lost his trail and he ventured to go to Chicago. Again he had Betty come to see him. They stayed at the Windmere Hotel and were happy to be with each other. After he lost his beloved Bertie, Victor's love and affections all went out to his daughter. He wanted her with him as much as possible.

Roberta, now married to Doug Conner, went to Chicago to get her daughter and Victor stayed on, hoping to elude the Secret Service, who, he knew, were hot on his trail again. They had located Watts through an informer and finally they caught Lustig, not by their own strategy but also through an informer who revealed his whereabouts to the police. This 'other' informer was Doug Conner.

This time Victor Lustig gave up. He would fight no more and declared his guilt and that of William Watts. This time the Secret Service was not going to be outwitted and they sent him to the Tombs under strict supervision and surveillance. From here on his story goes, not as he planned it, but as the law of the United States decreed. With William Watts, he was convicted and sent to Alcatraz; the rock prison in the Pacific Ocean. He had escaped conviction so many times that the law apparently wanted to put the ocean between him and possible escape.

Victor Lustig, who had operated under many aliases in his lifetime, was arrested as Robert V. Miller, alias 'Count' Victor Lustig. He did it to protect his family; the Secret Service never knew that he had a wife and a daughter.

On December 9, 1935, in the District Court of the United States, southern district of New York, Victor Lustig was sentenced on two indictments to 20 years of imprisonment and fined $1000. Indictment 1 sentenced him for five years imprisonment for having escaped from the Federal House of Detention on September 1, 1935. Indictment 2 sentenced him on six counts for counterfeiting and conspiracy against the United States. Sentencing read as follows:

'Count 1, 15 years and fined $1000; count 2, 15 years; count 3, 10 years, count 4, 15 years; count 5, 15 years; count 6, 2 years; All six sentences to run concurrently, but the first indictment of 5 years to run consecutively, making a sentence of 20 years.'

The indictment of Robert V. Miller, with aliases, and William Watts, with aliases, read in part with regard to conspiracy against the United States: 'It was part of said conspiracy that William Watts, with aliases, would manufacture and prepare . . . plates and negatives for the manufacture of counterfeit notes and securities of various denominations . . . It was also part of the conspiracy that Robert V. Miller, with aliases, would thereafter visit various cities and places throughout the United States for the purpose of negotiating for the distribution of the obligations and notes manufactured. It was also part of the conspiracy that William Watts would change hide-outs from time to time so as to make discovery very difficult and that, if Robert V. Miller was apprehended, he would escape detention and William Watts would change his hide-out under a fictitious name.'

So 'Count' Victor Lustig, who never carried a gun and never swindled an honest man, was sent to a prison reserved for the country's most dangerous criminals and murderers, for counterfeiting.

EIGHTEEN

BETTY WAS 13 years old when her father was captured and sent to Alcatraz. Before the year was up she determined that she would go to see her father. Her mother was then married to Doug Conner and they were living in Southern California. Her mother and step-father took her to San Francisco to put her on the boat that would take her, a mere child, alone to the rock in the Pacific Ocean that housed the one she loved. It housed the one that Roberta loved too, but she was married now to a man who would not permit her to see him; to the man, still unknown to her, that had put her husband in that rocky fortress.

The boat ride was a miserable one for Betty. The day was foggy and all she could see was the rock that towered before her. The only bright spot on the trip came from the guard who drove her from the boat at the dock at Alcatraz up to the compound. When she told him whom she was going to see, he answered her:

"Oh, Miller. I know him. Everybody likes him. He keeps busy with books and things, when other men do nothing. They don't keep their minds clear. They just sulk. Yes, he's a good man, your father you say he is?"

When she walked through the metal detectors, the bells all went off. Men and women came running from all directions. How could this quiet little bobby soxer, 4'11" tall, ring the bells at Alcatraz?! They soon discovered that she was wearing a sweater with brass buttons, which had sounded the alarm. They were all kind to her and led her through long corridors with detours and windowless tunnel-like halls. She had chewed her finger nails all the way there. She knew her father hated that habit which she had as a child and she was planning her strategy now as they walked her through the dark corridors. She would grab him and hug him with her arms tight around his neck. And she would keep them there, around his neck, so that he would never see that her nails were chewed off again.

She began to feel sick. She was afraid she would throw up if these long dark corridors didn't stop pretty soon. She felt a pressure on her arm and looked up into the kindest face she had ever seen. A nice lady asked her if this was her first time there. When she said yes, the lady asked:

"Who is it, dear?"

"It's not an it! He's my father and I'm proud of him. He's handsome and I love him and they're picking on him," the little girl on her first visit to a prison replied vehemently.

The lady smiled kindly and hugged her. Then she saw her father. There he was standing up, his face pressed against the glass with a wire mesh inside. She couldn't touch him. He picked up a phone and motioned her to pick up the one on her side. She forgot all about her nails and pressed her right hand against the glass. He moved the phone to his left hand and pressed his right hand against hers on the other side of the glass. She started to cry when she heard his distorted voice over the phone. She turned around and saw a guard behind her.

"It doesn't work," she cried out to him. "That's not his voice."

The guard smiled and motioned Victor to the other end of the visitors' stalls. Betty ran to the end on her side. She began to weep violently and babbled to him.

"I love you Daddy. I love you so much. Get out of here."

Her father tried to tell her not to cry, that he was proud of her, that she was beautiful and looked like Judy Garland. He told her not to waste time crying, that he would be out some time and that he would take her to Europe with him.

"How is Buckle?" he asked.

"She loves you too, Daddy. Will you take her to Europe with us?" Victor just smiled and said nothing. He seemed older, but he still had his beautiful eyes. He motioned for Betty to put her face against the glass and he kissed her from his side. The guard stepped up and shook his head, "No."

The child turned on him and cried, "You are a nasty man!" The guard just walked away. She put her hands up again and her father said over the telephone, "Where are your finger nails?"

"I had them, honest I did Daddy, but I chewed them off on the way to San Francisco and on the boat coming over. I was so nervous."

"Please, don't be so nervous," he told her. "I want you to have beautiful hands for me so when I buy you a beautiful star sapphire you can wear it on beautiful hands."

"I don't want anything but you, Daddy," she said through her tears.

"I hope there won't be a war in Europe, Betty, or I won't be able to take you over there."

A bell rang and she knew their time was up. She cried harder than ever. He told her again he loved her and soon they would be together. The lady came over, smiled at Victor and put her arm around the girl as she led her away. He nodded at the lady, waved to Betty and she saw tears streaming down his face; the first time she had ever seen him shed tears. The guards on his side kept motioning with a billy-like club for him to leave. He backed away, smiling and waving to her. That was the last she saw of him, waving his handkerchief as he disappeared through the door on the other side of the gate. The lady pushed the child away to get her out into the corridor. She held on to her all through the dark halls and let her go only when Betty began running for the boat. All she could remember about the boat ride back was the damp air.

Conner and her mother were waiting for her when she landed. Conner was in the car. She greeted her mother:

"Mother, how could you have left my daddy and married that rotten man? I hate him."

She was determined to go to see her father again. This time she knew her step-father would never let her go, so she drew out a small savings she had and bought a round trip ticket to San Francisco on the bus. When she got there she couldn't get a pass to see her father. She was a minor and must have arrangements made by a parent. She had missed the return bus home and had no money to spend the night anyplace. She found a parked car at the side of the street with the door unlocked. She crawled in to sleep for the night. In her inexperience, she never thought of the bus station.

When a middle-aged woman got into the car a few hours later and started the motor, the girl and the woman both screamed. She jumped out. The driver went on and Betty spent the night on the grass in the park.

She got the bus the next morning and went home, determined that she would not live with her hated step-father any longer than she had to.

She began writing to her father and he wrote to her. Her step-father would not permit letters from him to come to their house, so Betty gave him Aunt Ethel's address to write her in Kansas. Because the letters were always delivered without the envelope to the prisoners, he never knew where she was living, and because half-aunt Ethel always opened the letters that came to Betty, Betty was never sure that she received all the letters that he wrote. However, she has 45 letters from him, written on prison stationery, one page on both sides always with the heading "Robert V. Miller to Miss Betty Jean Miller" and the date. They are all available for this study. A few other letters, written before his conviction are also preserved. One, dated February 10, 1932, after the second divorce, is filled with pathos for the daughter that had been taken from him.

"My dear little honey, Betty Jean."

"I am on my way far away and I only want to say good bye before I go. So, when you get big you can come to me, but always remember you have a daddy that loves you and always will, even if you never see him again. Good bye, darling. Be good. From your daddy who will never forget you."

On April 27, 1935, he wrote to her while she was in the convent boarding school:

"I received your lovely letter and the pictures. Even if they were small, I like them very much. I am glad you like the things. I am sending you some more this week. When you have time, make a list and let me know what sizes in gloves, dresses, and all other things. It is hard to guess as you are growing like an Indian."

"I will try and get you a leopard coat for this winter as I know you have always wanted one. I would like to see you in your Easter outfit. You say I will be proud of you when you get big. I think you were wrong. I was proud of you when you were little and am proud of you now. I love you just as you are and always will. I think of you many times but I just have to be satisfied to think. Perhaps some day when you understand better, it may make a lot of difference. Don't think, honey, just because I don't see you, you must know by now that I love you. I will come to see you sure in June. It is so far away but don't forget I have made many long trips just to see you, if only for an hour. Someday you and I will have lots of time together."

But it took imprisonment on a damp and humid rock in the Pacific Ocean to reveal the other side of a very composite character, to reveal the kind of man he could have been had he not taken the wrong road when friends tried to persuade him to lead a lawful life; or to go back farther, had a proud father not broken a violin over a young boy's head.

NINETEEN

A T ALCATRAZ IN the 30's, when prison conditions consisted mainly of murders and violence, Victor Lustig lived a peaceful life. No one ever assaulted him or used violence against him.

For a time, Robert V. Miller was assigned to the library at Alcatraz. Letters to his daughter reveal his life there and how he spent his time. He also worked in the yard and wrote in one letter: "It keeps me outside all day and I like it . . . I watch the boats and lately a lot of airplanes including the Clipper every week. I can see almost 30 miles out through the Golden Gate and when I see a plane leaving in the daytime, I wish the pilot luck, even though he can't hear me. I work a little in the morning and play bridge in the afternoon."

How this wild adventurous man, born too early to ride the planes as often as we do today, must have envied the pilots who could fly through the skies. He would have something in the skies to conquer or swindle too.

His daughter has in her possession two large scrap books which he made while working in the library at Alcatraz and which the warden sent to her after his death. One scrap book is a photo study of world history. He made the scrap book under difficult conditions, constructing the cover and pages himself, using flour and water for paste. Pictures telling the story of civilization start '8000 years ago' he wrote in a letter, and continue through Caesar, Charlemagne, the Middle Ages, the Renaissance, modern times, both World Wars. He 'pictures' world leaders of all modern countries and American history in detail. He wrote once that he had 6000 pictures and was not nearly through.

A second scrap book which Betty has in her possession is devoted to family pictures; a photo album of Roberta and Betty. It contains the pictures that Betty sent him regularly during the years at Alcatraz. Some, perhaps, he had in his possession when he was convicted and they were not taken away from him. Another inmate, an artist, colored the pictures for him. Again, he constructed the scrap book to hold pictures of his family from the time he first met his wife and their child was born.

He was paid small sums of money for good behavior and for work he did. Betty received receipts to the amount of approximately $400.00. There were probably many more which she did not have. He used the money which he received, usually four or five dollars at a time to buy war bonds for Betty and his first grandchild. He had much information about CARE, which had been formed to send food packages to famine-stricken Europe after the war. No doubt he sent such packages, for the name of Gertrude Lustig, his half-sister, was among the addresses mentioned in the packet. A note in his handwriting to Betty says: "I have plenty money when I get out for you and myself only." He may have been referring to a deposit box he had in a Chicago City Bank, paid for 20 years; such information was on another scrap of paper sent with his effects to his daughter after his death.

He feared the Second World War, which he saw coming and which he said would be a terrible thing. In a letter dated June 2, 1941, he wrote: "I think this country will be in war in two months and I guess there is no question about it. It will make it bad for my release (he was hoping for release and deportation, since he was not an American citizen). It looks like the war may last five years or longer. With all the millions of people over there suffering, the people of this country should not complain."

He hated war and wanted peace and freedom for every human being, including himself. He saw the forces that would bring on World War II, followed its every detail in his reading in the library at Alcatraz and dreamed of a world that would have peace as its goal.

Among the effects sent to Betty after his death was his peace plan. Along with the peace plan was a file of clippings concerning peace proposals that were being made at the end of the war, the Dunbarton Oaks plan, the formation of the United Nations, and world security. He must have studied them all and then written his own, which, he wrote, he thought was simpler than any other proposal.

German forces were weakening when Lustig wrote his peace plan and he saw the policing of Germany as the first big job of the international court. He thought it might be done best by the German people themselves if they recognized the law and knew that they would be responsible if they made any renewed effort at war. After the disarmament of Germany, the immobilizing of millions of soldiers would save millions of dollars.

"The majority of Germans would want to live in peace and would not hesitate to denounce any secret war plant above or underground," he said, "especially when it would be as simple as notifying the nearest United Nations Embassy. It would be much easier to enforce this law by the German people themselves and their police force than by a lot of United Nation military troops, which would only cause resentment."

He concluded his peace plan by saying, "The fact that I have lived in Germany a long time convinces me that my ideas about this international law would be worth while investigating. I have many more additional suggestions but have stated here only the main principles."

It took Alcatraz and years of confinement to induce Victor Lustig to use his God-given intelligence for some worthy cause like the peace plan. The policing of Victor Lustig proved to be a bigger task than policing the world.

Along with the peace plan which was sent from Alcatraz to Victor Lustig's daughter, came a handwritten article titled 'Verboten'. It was a plan for the policing of Germany after the war. Lustig saw Germany as the world's problem and wrote in this article his plan to take care of Germany and remove the occupation forces from the country, saving millions of dollars and enabling the conquering countries to remove thousands of their forces from the country. His whole unique plan as outlined in 'Verboten' is worth quoting in parts.

"The word 'Verboten' in the German language is sacred. There is no person in Germany who has not seen, read, or heard of it. Translated into English, it means 'forbidden'. Anybody who has never lived in or visited Germany will not realize how important and vital this word is in German. 'Verboten' signs are found in almost every house, school, church, store, and park; and in every hamlet, village, city and state in Germany. These signs are printed on the most durable material. They range in sizes from three inches by five inches to three feet by five feet, usually set in a wooden frame. When you read that something is 'verboten', it means just that and it is to be strictly observed. Only in isolated cases is the rule ignored."

"There is another word in German which is very important and second only in importance to 'verboten' and this word is 'belohnung' or 'reward'! It will be posted everywhere and read mostly by persons who would like to increase their income by a few extra dollars (marks). This word 'belohnung' or 'reward' is used in cases where certain persons are wanted by the authorities for the crime of murder, robbery, jewel theft, or to apprehend known thieves and criminals . . . ."

"The reason I have thoroughly explained and stressed these two vital and well-known words, especially the first word 'verboten', is because it will play the main part in the peace plan."

"Peace plan translated into German means 'friedens plan'. In our enforcement of it, in Germany, we will use the two words together and post them in every factory, workshop, public building, school, church, store, train, street car, bus, etc.; in every hamlet, town city, and state. There are also the facilities of the radio. Peace Plan or Friedens Plan could or should be made a slogan and broadcast as 'Friedens Plan Pour Deutschland'."

"Any person who takes part, open or secret, in any 'bund' or organization of troop training of a war-like gesture; Any person who willfully works secretly in any organization where war materials are being manufactured shall be working against the 'Friedens Plan' and will be dealt with according to the law; punishment to be meted out from one month to life imprisonment, the punishment to be decided by an International Tribunal Council."

"Any person who shall report a person or persons who have violated any of the rules or laws laid down by the International Tribunal Council will be rewarded, 'belohnung,' the sum of from $5 to $500 . . ."

"There are many reasons for these two signs, 'verboten' and 'belohnung'. The German people will be reminded, many times each day, that only through their honest cooperation will they be permitted to regain their position in the United Nations councils."

"It is a well-known fact to those who have studied the psychology of the German people that they are great believers in signs and posters . . . A German will go out of his way to read a sign and even be more willing to obey, for it is his nature to obey."

He then goes into detail to show how much man power could be saved in the German occupation, reducing the entire occupation forces to 2,500 which he shows will be adequate when the people themselves are enforcing the laws through the posting of the two signs.

"I select Berlin as the headquarters of the 'supreme enforcement agency' from which there is no appeal as in our supreme court. All minor offenses could be acted upon in the locality in which they occur. All major cases could be decided upon in headquarters in Berlin."

"This small force of 2,500 men," he says, "appears to be inadequate for the task they are to perform. But owing to Germany's excellent communications, it will be seen that whenever an unpleasant situation arises, a force of any number of these 2,500 men could be sent to investigate within an hour's time. For example, if an unpleasant situation should arise in Bernburg, the forces in the cities of Leipzig, Holle and Chemnitz, which have 16 men at their disposal, could reach Bernberg in an hour's notice. As time goes on this force could be reduced to as low as 200 men, if everything runs smoothly."

He was speaking for the American Occupation Forces, but he adds that if all the occupation forces of other countries would cooperate, a grand total of 22,000 men is the most that would ever be needed.

TWENTY

I N HIS FIRST letter from prison, from Leavenworth where he was incarcerated before being sent to Alcatraz, dated February 8, 1936, Victor Lustig said this to his daughter:

"My dearest Betty,

Received your letter and also five dollars. Thanks very much. Am very glad you are O.K . . . . You probably think I have forgotten your birthday. I have not and as long as I can't say it with flowers or some other present, I will say it with a poem. I have made it all myself and even though it is not as artistic as Shakespeare would have written it, it is only for you, so you have to be satisfied as it is.

B irthday memories while thinking of you
E ager and happy wishing for you
T he happiness that could not be sold
T omorrow you be 14 years old
Y our birthday alone counts in the world,

I hope you will get this on or before your birthday so you would not think I have forgotten you. When you have time, think of me as I think of you. Let me know how you like my poetry and when you will see me, tell me . . . You can come this month.

So write soon and wishing you a happy birthday and many of them, I will close with all my love and a million kisses. My best to the folks. Always, your daddy.

Robert V. Miller
(48065)"

Through his work in the library, Lustig was able to keep up with what was going on in literature, science, medicine, industry. He wrote in one letter to his daughter that Hemingway seemed to be the writer of the day. He spoke of ordering some books to read and asked his daughter to tell him what she was reading and, if they had them in the library at Alcatraz, he would read them too and they could discuss them in later letters.

He wrote about a new drug that had been developed that could combat almost every disease. He was no doubt referring to sulfa and the discovery of antibiotics in the 30's. He wrote her once that he had read about color photography that was then being developed and thought it would be easy to make a dark room to develop color pictures. Betty had gotten interested in photography and he wanted to help her. He suggested that some relative, who, Betty told him, was in the automobile business, should get into planes. They were the coming things.

He wrote, "Talking about photography dark rooms, do you realize what tremendous things have developed in that line? The latest is they can take a picture in a dark spot without flashlights. Try this when you want a fine picture. To get an excellent picture depends on proper exposure . . ." He goes on to explain in detail how to avoid under and over exposure, how to prepare the development solution, and how to get depth in the picture. He would have told her more, he said, but he had no more room to write. They were limited to one page of paper on both sides and he had his space filled up.

He kept up on the war in every detail and was surprised that Betty did not talk about it. He felt that Americans did not take it seriously and he knew it was a very serious affair. He wrote: "I have time to read now and I am following the war closely. I predict that Russia will dictate the peace. Any country that has 90 percent illiteracy and in 10 years became 90 percent literate is going to dictate to the other countries. Too bad Germany broke with Russia. Germany, Russia and Japan could have ruled the world."

In a letter dated November 25, 1942, he wrote: "The old tradition they call war is like a trade; it must be learned. You can see why the democracies at first did so poorly. My opinion, regardless of most writers and poll takers including some military men, is that Germany will collapse in two years. Japan is not easy but will not last much longer and Russia can't be conquered. I predict the United States will be in Tripoli before New Years."

Victor asked prison officials if he could be transferred to some place where he could see his daughter. He asked her to write to James Bennett, Director of Prisons, Washington, D.C. and ask if he could be transferred. They do it occasionally, he said.

The war went on and Victor Lustig continued to write to his daughter, following the war, predicting peace and assuring his daughter of his love for her. She was having marital troubles and was trying to avoid telling her father about it. He wrote: "Your letter seems very confusing, just like one of those continued stories you read which is not completed. Like, the boat tipped over in the ocean and the people are in the water. We do not know whether they are drowned or rescued, continued next month. I like to read mystery stories but not in a letter from you." In his next letter, after she had told more of her trouble, he apologized for the light way he had written her.

He wrote many more letters, always signed 'With all my love, always your daddy #300 Robert V. Miller.' He wrote weekly, always cheerful. He tells of the good dinners they had on Christmas and New Years and the movies they were shown. Once he wrote suggesting names for the baby Betty was expecting. "I think Thelma Geraldine would be nice or Marjorie Helen. I don't think much of Judy, even though Judy Garland is famous and Judith was a famous Hebrew heroine. It would be like naming a boy Aladin because of Aladin's wonderful lamp." When Betty wrote that she had named the baby Kathleen, he told her it was a beautiful name.

He still hoped for release and was sure he would have been paroled if it had not been for the war. "But I mustn't complain," he wrote. "With all the people suffering in Europe, one cannot think of himself."

Again he wrote, "I have been planning that as soon as the war is over I want you and your husband to see all of Europe. I should be able to be your guide. There will be a lot of people going and I want to show you all the places you want to see . . . I will be released in 38 months, even if the war is still on. I know it is still a long time but it is the best I can do."

In an earlier letter he had written Betty that when he would be released, he would never do anything wrong again. "I promise you, Skeezix, and I always keep my promises." Finally at Alcatraz, Victor Lustig realized his greatness and, too late, showed the other side of a very humane and kind man.

He tells her in a letter dated April 17, 1946, that he can be released or deported in another year. He could ask for parole after seven years, he says, but the war had interfered here and now he prefers release and deportation to parole . . . He thinks he might be able to shorten his time by earning extra good time, that he had been making five extra hours every month. He speaks again of his promise of employment as an interpreter by the minister of Czechoslovakia.

He told Betty repeatedly not to come to see him. They couldn't get together and it only made them both feel bad because of the visit. Shortly after that he wrote that he was in the hospital, nothing serious. Betty wrote: "I am still planning and I will not change my plans to go to see you. When, I can't say. Kathy has a cold and I will not leave her until she is well. I may have to wait until mother gets here so I will have someone to leave her with."

TWENTY-ONE

ROBERTA NEVER GAVE up the idea, all the years that Victor was at Alcatraz, that money could free him. She decided to sell the story of his life. Victor had never permitted this to be done. He had had many offers, but always declined because of his family. Now Roberta was determined to go ahead in spite of his refusals to sell his story. It would save his life now and that was all that concerned her, not her own or her daughter's protection.

She looked for a writer. She wrote to Lionel Moise, now a Hearst journalist in New York, whom she had stood up the night she met Victor. Moise was bitter for many years, but time had softened his resentment and she had had enough contact with him to think that he might consider her request. His reply was disappointing.

"Dear Bertie:

Your letter was forwarded to me promptly, but I haven't had a chance to answer until now.

I know Betty must be a darling if she's half as pretty and dynamic as her mother. I'm sure you haven't changed either. Anyway, don't tell me if you have.

Sorry I can't offer you any competition – I never fancied myself in the role of a father, you know. More the daddy type if you know what I mean.

About the manuscript, I'd like to, but I'm afraid it's out of the question. Right now I have twice as many necessary jobs to do every day as I have time and energy for. I couldn't possibly take on anything else, for money or even for love.

After all, Bertie, I am a couple hundred years old at least and I have to treat myself gently to keep from falling apart. Whoops. Almost dropped an arm off just then.

Life is pretty dull these days. Nobody tries to shoot me or tear me apart and I like it that way. Not reformed, Mrs. Conner, just tired.

I'll give you a ring next time I am in L.A. and you can see for yourself. I'm only sorry I can't look after the literary matter.

Love and things,
Lionel."

She wrote to Walter Winchell. Walter wanted her to write the story and he would sell it for her. Roberta now found herself thwarted in this plan to free her husband. All the time she was married to Doug Conner, she still felt that Victor was her husband. She would never feel differently.

She wouldn't give up. She sold her jewelry; expensive pieces which Victor had given her through the years and amassed $70,000. She went to see James Bennett, Director of Prisons who was in Los Angeles. She came home and wept. $70,000 was not enough to free Victor.

In the meantime, Victor at Alcatraz was making every effort to secure his probation, to see that nothing would stand in the way should probation be granted him. His years at Alcatraz as gleaned from his letters, had been calm ones; working in the library, keeping himself busy and keeping in touch with world events. Among the effects sent to his daughter from Alcatraz after his death, we find, besides scrap books mentioned earlier, the following list: book, 'Sonnets from the Portuguese'; book 'Der Fuehrer'; one Winston simplified dictionary; two folders; French lessons from the University of California; one folder containing literature about CARE (He sent CARE packages to war victims as often as his small earnings allowed); one folder marked, 'Peace Plan'. All of this shows the length and breadth of his interests, when his genius was no longer at work on illegal schemes.

But now, his last days at Alcatraz, his whole interest seemed to be put into efforts to secure his probation and deportation to his native country.

He wrote to the Office Clerk, Bedford, Massachusetts:

"Dear Sir:

I was arrested in Paris, France, in June or July, 1929, and held in Paris for three months. After that, some of your men came after me and had a Washington extradition warrant against me. I was extradited on the ship 'George Washington' to your town and held for trial. The case was for defrauding Mr. Thomas Burns of $45,000. I got out on a $15,000 bail put up by a New York Company. I have a detainer from your office and the immigration has a detainer for me to be shipped to Europe.

I hope you can let me go as I am today about 58 years old and have been sentenced to Alcatraz prison for 20 years. My sentence will expire this July. I have several injuries that will remain permanently. I hope you can let me go."

He wrote to the man who had been his attorney in the Bedford case. He was confused whether it was Bedford or New Bedford, Massachusetts.

"Dear Mr. Serpa," he wrote. "I expect to be released from Alcatraz prison in the near future and would like to know certain details of the case pending against me since 1929 in New Bedford. I do not remember the name under which I was extradited from Paris to New Bedford. Be so kind as to let me know."

"As you know there were certain persons involved with me in this case and I would like to know what has happened to these co-defendants. Also would like to know what happened to the $15,000 bond posted with the New York bonding company."

"Will you please be so kind as to determine and to forward me such information as you may be able to secure pertaining to my present status in this case. Also would like to have any documents relative to this matter and to know where I can find an international treaty between France and the United States on which I was extradited in November, 1929."

"Hoping to hear from you at your earliest convenience, I am

Very truly yours,

Robert V. Miller
Alcatraz, California"

This letter was returned to him with the notification that there was no such person at the time residing in New Bedford.

The damp, cold climate at Alcatraz was affecting his health. His sinus condition, which he had suffered since childhood, was worsening and he feared for his endurance until he could be released. He asked to be transferred to a prison in a milder climate and wrote to Mr. Tom Clark, the Attorney General of the United States:

"Dear Sir:

I have for the past two years attempted to obtain a transfer from Alcatraz to a milder type institution and I earnestly believe in my eligibility for such a transfer. My inability to obtain this transfer, along with Warden Johnson's suggestion to present my case to you, have prompted me to solicit your intercession on my behalf.

Warden Johnson has spoken well of my conduct and record in general while here and he has told me in a recent interview that I deserved a transfer.

I have written the director, Mr. Bennett and I have had interviews with him. He speaks favorably and encouragingly but will make no definite statement.

I am a man 57 years old and my health has deteriorated a great deal in the past five years. I suffer from asthma, bronchitis, and a sinal condition. You can readily see that this climate is not very conducive to my physical well being. If I was transferred inland my condition would undergo a rapid improvement. Also, Mr. Clark, I wish to apply for a deportation parole and have purposely delayed submitting my application, knowing that the stigma of the institution might prejudice the parole board. Warden Johnston has concurred with me in the belief that I should wait until it is possible to apply from a more favorable place.

I have written the Secret Service Department and the sentencing judge and they say they will offer no objection to my parole, C. Jan Mazoryk, minister of Czechoslovakia, has stated, on occasion of my letter, that I have a good chance of obtaining employment as an interpreter with the Czech government upon my release.

I have been at Alcatraz 11 years, which leaves me about 16 months still to serve. This is my first conviction and I received the maximum sentence; a deportation warrant has been placed against me and I will be deported to my native Czechoslovakia upon release. Considering my record while here together with my age and the above facts, it is my honest belief that transferring me to a milder type institution would be in keeping with the policy of your Bureau of Prisons.

I am very fortunate in that I speak, read, and write fluently all the European languages and dialects. The situation being that it is in Europe assures me of a job when I arrive there. My advanced years and my impaired health all favor this type of employment and it is inconceivable that the Parole Board would not consider these facts in passing upon my approbation for a deportation parole.

I am enclosing the letter I have from Mr. Jan Masouryk; also I am enclosing a letter which I would like to have permission to mail. This letter was written sometime ago but not mailed because of prematurity.

In conclusion, Mr. Clark, I want to emphasize that this is not a letter from a disgruntled prisoner; but a petition from one who honestly believes in his eligibility for a transfer, and one who only asks that you consider my record, the facts I have stated, and whatever else that is necessary for a just decision.

It is my sincere hope, Mr. Clark, that you will find that I do merit a transfer; and I am confident that you will do what is necessary to see that my case is dealt with in fairness.

Very respectfully yours"

We do not know whether this appeal ever arrived at the office of the Attorney General or not. It is undated and written on scratch paper. And there is no record of an answer from Mr. Clark. It was the final appeal of a sincere but desperate man for his freedom.

All of these efforts for release on Victor Lustig's part and Betty's efforts to go to visit him as soon as her mother arrived to care for her baby did not fructify.

On December 5, 1946, Betty received a letter from Warden Johnson at Alcatraz saying her father was critically ill. She was more determined than ever to go to see him. Would her mother ever arrive? Then on December 11 another letter came.

> "Dear Madam:
>
> In my letter to you of December 5, 1946, it was with regret that I had to inform you that your father, Robert V. Miller. was critically ill in the hospital here.
>
> Today upon the advice from the chief medical officer, I am very happy to let you know that his condition is very much improved and the outlook for his recovery is most encouraging. Of course active treatment will be necessary for an indefinite time, but should anything unforeseen develop, we will advise you."

Complications arising from her mother's delay in arriving and the baby's illness kept Betty from going to Alcatraz and the letter just quoted was reassuring enough for her to delay her trip until after Christmas.

She began negotiations, by all possible means, to have him released to her and her mother in Los Angeles. Time for his probation was only months away and it would cost the government nothing to have them care for him. But it was all to no avail. The transfer which did come was not what she expected.

A letter dated January 2, 1947, came saying that her father had been transferred to the United States Medical Center in Springfield, Missouri. The tone of the letter, however, was reassuring as it said that a medical representative from the Bureau of Prisons had been there and, since the patient had been making progress and was deemed able to travel, it was recommended that he be transferred. From California, Springfield was farther away than Alcatraz.

Betty delayed going to see her father until a Western Union telegram, dated March 4, 1947, read: 'Your father, Robert V. Miller, is considered critically ill.' She delayed no longer. But how would she get there? In those after-war days, it was almost impossible to get a seat on a plane on quick notice. They were all too busy transporting soldiers. She certainly did not have a priority which was necessary to cut the red tape. She appealed to a good friend, Vic Genco, who was transportation manager for Weber Showcase and he got her a reservation, at the risk of his job, as Betty Weber.

Arriving in Springfield, she registered at the Colonial Hotel. She had very little money and staying at the hotel, even the lowest rates, would be difficult. Contrary to what people thought, Betty and her mother had very little money now and depended for their living on Betty's work and money from the sale of Roberta's jewels from the earlier days as Victor's wife. Roberta did own a beautiful little home in the better part of Los Angeles and furnishings from the past, kept well and new looking, surprised most of their friends. Few knew the pockets were nearly empty. It was a mystery how Roberta and Betty always dressed well, a mystery no one ever solved. Once a friend asked "Bertie, how do you and Betty do it? You both dress well, the house is perfect, your furniture looks like new, just how do you manage?" Bertie glanced at Betty, smiled and said "That's for us to know and you to try and find out, but I'll tell you something for sure, we 'come by it' honest."

When Betty saw her father she knew that she had waited too long. He was paralyzed and could not talk. An operation at Alcatraz, the doctors said, had resulted in the paralysis. 'Why operate in such a manner for sinus?' she said over and over in her fury and despair to find her father in this condition. She must communicate with him and she knew how she could. She took his hand in hers and gently tapped on his palm as she whispered in his ear 'Morse Code'. She tapped in Morse Code in preference to whispering, "I love you, Daddy." Feebly, with a strained smile in those large, expressive eyes, he tapped back. "I love you, too, Skeezix."

Many more messages followed each day as she returned from the hotel to spend as much time as they allowed with him, with security, of course, looking on most of the time. "How is your mother?" "How is the baby?" "Why didn't you answer all my letters?" and Betty's answers: "Mother loves you, Daddy. She has forgiven you. She has tried to get you out of prison. She has done everything she could."

His eyes were unbelieving now but she continued to assure him that he was forgiven, that she would come to see him but she was taking care of his granddaughter, there was no one else to do it. When his hands got too weak to tap out messages, she smuggled in a small slate under a heavy knit sweater, had marked the alphabet in large letters on it and gave him a pointer. She held the pointer in his hand and supported his hand while he indicated the letter he wanted. He would point to L-O-V-E, it was all he could manage, so back to the Morse Code.

He began to repulse everyone but Betty, pushed them aside with his good left arm and would throw off the covers. Only Betty could calm him. He would hold her hand tightly and when her time of visiting was over, it took time to ease away gently. Once he motioned for the guard to come to him and with much effort and pointing, made him understand that he must take care of Betty and see that no harm came to her from the prisoners walking in the halls. The guard figured her father feared someone might try to use Betty as a hostage.

On the evening of March 11 when Betty was leaving him, she stood in the doorway and waved at him, "I'll be back in the morning, Daddy, early."

He smiled with his tired eyes. "I'll be here Daddy. I promise. Auf wiedersehn." His eyes followed her out of the door.

She turned again and looked back. They were giving him oxygen. It was the last time she was to see him alive. Early, shortly before dawn, they called her at the hotel and told her that her father had died during the night.

On March 12, 1947, she made the following affidavit: 'I Elizabeth Schwartz, certify that I am the daughter of Robert V. Miller, deceased, and desire to claim his body for burial in Kansas City, Missouri. Please prepare and ship his body to Quirk and Tobin funeral home, corner Linwood and Main Streets, Kansas City, Missouri. Permission for post mortem examination is refused.'

Again, she used a name that was not hers.

She made arrangements with Quirk and Tobin in Kansas City to receive the body and went to Kansas City with him. She had insisted she would not leave him alone even if they had to ride in separate sections.

If her heart had been broken successively by his imprisonment, his illness, his death, this was the final, most tragic blow. The body arrived from Springfield in a pine box with an orange makeup on his face and a celluloid collar stapled in such a way one end of a staple had penetrated the flesh of his neck. Quirk and Tobin, however, did a remarkable job of restoring Victor's dignity.

Betty had him buried in Mt. Moriah cemetery with Roberta's blanket of roses covering his new and beautiful casket. He was dressed in all new clothing purchased from the best store in Kansas City, nothing was left undone.

TWENTY-TWO

VICTOR LUSTIG'S DEATH at the Prison Medical Center in Springfield did not reach the news media for two years. His wife and daughter began new lives. Betty, a child of luxury and devoted to a father who returned all of her love, to a life of work making a living for her two daughters; and Roberta, divorced from her second husband, Doug Conner, to a life of guilt and self castigation for having brought on the death of her husband.

She had learned that Doug Conner, while still married to her, had been the 'informer' who alerted the Secret Service about the whereabouts of Victor. Always jealous of his wife's first husband, he had finally succeeded in tracing his whereabouts to Chicago. Roberta had always been very careful not to let him know where Victor was, but this time Roberta's sister Mae told Doug that Roberta was going to Chicago to see Victor. Always the troublemaker, Mae also succeeded in hurting Roberta, but didn't realize she would be hurting Victor who had been the gift giver of the family. So Doug Conner secretly followed Roberta to Chicago when she went there to bring Betty home from her visit with her father. Conner then alerted the Secret Service.

Emil Lustig, proud old Ludwig Lustig's second disappointment, leaked the news of his brother's death in the Springfield Medical Center when he himself had been arrested on a counterfeit charge. His disclosure, he thought, would help to gain his release on a personal bond. Not so, it served no useful purpose and he knowingly revealed something the family did not want known.

Victor Lustig had brought his brother to the United States on a forged passport after he had deserted the Germany Army and was awaiting execution. He escaped with help from Vic. Emil, at times, had been his brother's accomplice in the United States and had helped him occasionally, for he too was an actor like his brother and could help pull off capers creditably. But he was unreliable, did not have the ability that his brother had and never brought an undertaking to fulfillment. He married a good woman, Louise Lustig, and her name appears often in family gatherings through the years. Emil spent his last days with friends or relations, living off their bounty and straining their efforts to practice charity.

After Emil's disclosure that his brother was dead, newspapers carried stories about the 'Count' from New York to the West Coast. Headlines read: 'Death of Notorious Swindler Disclosed', 'Count Lustig, Counterfeiter, Died in Prison, Brother Reveals', 'Death of Notorious Swindler Bared', and so on.

All of them told of his life as counterfeiter, about his 'money box' and the number of times he was arrested but never convicted because he could always buy his way out. But no writer ever mentioned he was survived by a wife and daughter. The well-guarded secret by the old-time writers, that Victor had a family, was never revealed. Walter Winchell refused to report Victor's death and would certainly never reveal there was a family. Victor's many friends, among them leading motion picture stars, could have done well to avail themselves of the press to seek publicity. Although never agreeing with Lustig's way of life, they always guarded it and saved Roberta and Betty from blackmail or kidnapping. Victor's ability to make friends and to keep them was as uncanny as his whole life story.

Money began coming to Roberta and Betty, unsigned, or from a friend 'whom your husband helped'. It came from many cities and resort areas, too late to help Victor but in time to help Roberta and Betty, who could no longer go to a lock box in all the large cities of the country and withdraw all the money they needed. One letter had a typed message fastened to the top of a $500 bill. It read:

'My father would want me to send you this. Vic helped him out and never would accept repayment.'

Another letter, unsigned, contained $10,000, which kept them alive and paid their bills for some time.

But there also came different kinds of letters to Betty from fellow prisoners of her father at Alcatraz. Some were written before Victor died, with Victor's name signed to his darling Betty Jean. She knew they were spurious, for they were written after her father had the stroke and he could not possibly have told them to write or dictated to them. Others wrote after his death and offered sympathy and help. One writer, named Peter, said he had some valuable information to give her that her father had told him before he left Alcatraz. He must see her to tell her this most important thing that it was necessary for her to know. They were all desperate men who had envied Lustig and his daughter, men reaching from their stony fortress for someone to love them, someone they could touch, and feel that they were not abandoned by mankind. But Betty did not feel that she could take them all on.

Another man named Charlie Lang, wrote her warning her against one of those who were writing her from prison. This man, Jim, Charlie told her, had been forgotten by family and friends and wanted someone who would contact him, send him money for tobacco, etc. Betty found out that her father had befriended

Charlie Lang, had brought him from Berlin and helped him get a start. Roberta remembered and liked Charlie. He was working now as a waiter in New York and began sending Betty money until she told him to stop. He needed it more than she did, she was sure. It all taught her that a prison ministry was what all prisoners, no matter how great their crimes, yearned for.

TWENTY-THREE

Endowed with much of his charm, Victor Lustig's daughter found it easy to secure rewarding jobs. Her spotty education with tutors and short terms in some 37 schools had always been too interrupted to prepare her for a profession or a career. To get away from a hated step-father, she married while she was still very young. Now twice divorced with two young children, she taught herself typewriting and read a medical dictionary. She became a medical secretary to a Beverly Hills, California, cardiologist and was able to support herself and children. Roberta, divorced from Doug Conner, was selling more and more of her valuables to keep up the life style she had enjoyed as the wife of Victor Lustig. She had two friends, both elderly gentlemen for whom she dressed every day. When they died, she had no one to dress for. She was nearing 70 years of age, her health began to fail. She was threatened with blindness. Her feet and legs were so swollen she could no longer wear her 4½ size shoes and she felt that no efforts could ever again salvage her appearance. When she knew positively that her second husband, Doug Conner, was the informant who destroyed her Vic, she fed on guilt. She had destroyed him by marrying Conner.

Betty, as Jeanne De Noret, (the name Lustig was still too much of a risk) had gone from medical secretary to hotel business. That was certainly the business that she could feel most at home in, for she had lived in hotels most of her life. She became executive secretary to the manager of the new Hilton Hale Kaanapali Hotel in Maui, Hawaii. Next she went to New York to train for a position as manager for a major hotel chain in St. Thomas, Virgin Islands. But after her first month of employment at what could have been the beginning of a fine career, a telephone call brought her back to the West to care for her mother, who was threatened with cancer and was aging fast. Selfish and pampered all of her life, she was selfish now in her older days and insisted that her daughter be with her.

One week before she died, Roberta called Betty Jean to her and said she wanted to talk about the future. It should have been a premonition to her daughter, but it wasn't. She kept insisting that the future was still far off and there was nothing to worry about. They sat and talked quietly.

"Promise me, Betty," her mother said, "that you will bury me beside Vic. And, Betty, I don't want to be buried where he is. I hate that city. All the hard things of my life happened there."

She took both Betty Jean's hands in hers and, with tears streaming down her cheeks, she begged:

"Promise me, won't you. I'll be buried beside Vic. You'll do it somehow, won't you?"

The daughter was struggling with the thought of losing her mother and kept insisting she could live many more years. The mother put her arms around her child and kept whispering, "Promise me, promise me, Betty, for my peace of mind, promise me that I can lie beside my Vic."

"Sure, mother, I'll do anything you want, but let's not talk about it now."

"I knew you would, darling. You know we have to plan things ahead so we can put them out of our minds. And now I have your promise that I will be beside Vic."

Betty Jean assured her mother that it would be done, that she would begin now to see about bringing her father to where they were.

"Look into it right away, honey. Bring him home."

The next morning, worn out by grief and fear of the impending suffering from the cancer that threatened her, Roberta Lustig took an overdose of barbiturates and died, secure in the thought that she would lie beside her Victor.

Betty Jean, faced with a burial place for her mother and the promise that her father would lie beside her, began hurriedly to make plans. She ruled out the thought of taking her mother's body back to Kansas City, where her father was buried. Instead, she found a beautiful spot, a quiet cemetery far away from city noises and had her mother buried there. Then, she began cutting the red tape of five states to have her father brought there, so that the two, Roberta and Victor, could be there, side by side.

ADDENDUM

Betty Jean came to my town one summer many years ago. She was struggling with cancer and hoped to spend the rest of her days here. Through a mutual friend, I met her and soon we formed one of those friendships that happen so infrequently. As each of us had grown up in a small Kansas town, we spent many hours that summer talking and enjoying the other's company. She had lived a fascinating life, one that I had only read about in books.

Owing to circumstances and the heat of the summer, she decided she could not stay as she had planned. Betty returned to Las Vegas in the fall of that year driving her white Thunderbird convertible, still looking very glamorous. She passed away only a few short weeks later. Her greatest wish was to have her father's story told. She gave her mother's diary and notes to a mutual friend to record the story in manuscript form. It was finished after her death. Now, as Betty and the friend are now deceased, the task has passed down to me and one other. As I enter the sunset of my life, I am pleased fulfill her desire and my promise.

Looking back now, I realize that there were no pictures; she never mentioned any. Perhaps that was in keeping with the lifestyle she lived. She and her second husband are buried in Las Vegas. My promise kept, I shall visit her again, soon.

–Nanci Garrett, 2011

I MET BETTY JEAN in the early part of the 1980's. She had come to a small town in Kansas to spend the remaining days of her life after being diagnosed with terminal cancer. I was just out of my teens, full of myself and had no conception of this strong, resolute woman or her life experiences. I remember a large car, an elegant lady and a pampered Pekinese named 'Peekie'. She was befriended there by Ms. Garret and a few others. Through these friends, she attempted to define the man many had only a negative impression of. Using the scattered notes and Roberta's journal, they pieced together the narrative of the Lustig's lives together. Shortly thereafter, Betty packed and moved again for her 'final time' due to circumstances I and others are unwilling to relate here.

Betty Jean died in Las Vegas and was buried next to the only other man she truly loved, her husband who had passed a few years before. Upon her death, her final furry child was shipped back to Ms. Garret to live out his life, with friends, in the state of her birth. I remember 'Peekie' and can assure you, he was loved and cared for tenderly the rest of his days.

The story above is one of boundless love and devotion; of a father for a daughter, of a daughter for her father and of a couple for each other in the most unusual of circumstances. It is a love story so few know and far fewer have experienced, but all can be touched by. I am truly blessed to relate it to you now.

I have attempted to remain as faithful to the original document and prose in as much as possible. Any corrections I've made are minor (punctuation and shortening run-on sentences primarily), any further errors are my own. I pray she forgives me this arrogance and I do hope she would approve.

The road was so long, but rest now traveler.
For you are at home....
    ....with Buckle and Skeezits.

Rbt

While working on this project, I came across a copy of 'Hustlers and Con Men' by Jay Robert Nash, that Betty had owned. Inside, I found a rebuttal of sorts to what he had written about her father. I will reproduce it here with no edits.

Jay Robert Nash   (1976) ERRORS MARKED X THROUGHOUT

PRO AND CON   RE: NASH SEGMENTS IN THE BOOK HUSTLERS & CON MEN
This Pro-Con works with my calendar. Please refer to the calendar pages for notation.

PAGE #	Per Nash	My Response
98	Eiffel Tower - Twice sold	TRUE
117	Born in PRAGUE	FINALLY!
	"... worked his way to the US in early 1920's"	ON THIS I HAVE TO SAY IN ERROR More like 1918 or early 1919 – but it was *AFTER* WORLD WAR I And if he meant literally "worked his way" - not so - Grandfather paid – through the teeth – to see if possibly he would mend his ways.
	X CAPONE	WRONG
	X QUOTED AS SAYING: "Everything turns gray when I don't have at least one mark on the horizon . . ."	WRONG – no such attitude – he enjoyed everything in life – liked to take walks in the park, had many hobbies and many times "hurried" with a Mark so we could go on a peaceful vacation and he could mount those darned butterfly collections – he loved golf and went many times with Ty (Titanic T.) He just wasn't that shallow.
119	X Money box cost $15.00 to make	POO – the case alone cost $500.00
	X file – cell bars	NOPE – paid off guard – perhaps the guard made it look "good" and used a file – the guard walked him out through the kitchen – he hopped on a garbage truck and was met "outside" the gates by mother.
120	Sheriff Q.R. Miller	There's that name!
121	X Key in suitcase	Oh Lord – they can't get anything straight!
233	X I leave this job to you – I'll truly upchuck if I have to.	
234	X Now they have it 1922 in Paris Café re: Eiffel Tower! And large	
235	X BROWN eyes – thin BLOND hair – SABER SCAR OVER THE RIGHT EYEBROW!	
	X	
	X	
	X	
306 ?	1908	?
312	1922 Robert Duval	TRUE
316 X	CAPONE	NOPE
318	1930 abandons money box	VERY CLOSE TO TRUE
320	Yellow Kid mentioned and daddy arrested	TRUE
326	Dies	TRUE – but more like *murdered* by a surgeon

Lightning Source UK Ltd.
Milton Keynes UK
UKOW051525120312

188825UK00003B/161/P